THE ULTIMATE BOOK OF UNFORGETTABLE CREEPY CRAWLY JOKES

Compiled by Liz Hughes

Illustrated by Jazz Panesar

Robinson Children's Books

Robinson Publishing Ltd
7 Kensington Church Court
London W8 4SP

First published in the UK by Robinson Children's Books,
an imprint of Robinson Publishing Ltd, 1998

A copy of the British Library Cataloguing in Publication
Data for this title is available from the British Library.

ISBN 1 85487 869 7

Page Layout by Design 23, London

Printed and bound in the EC

10 9 8 7 6 5 4 3 2 1

CONTENTS

INTRODUCTION

This collection of creepy crawly jokes is truly unforgettable! Liz Hughes has included the widest possible selection of creepy things to laugh at. There are funnies about crawly things with legs, slimy things that slither, little brown things that hop, long silent things that slide, yellow striped things that buzz, and many more creepy crawly things that inch, ooze, drip, trickle, shuffle, flutter or trail their way along. But that's not all. The creepy selection extends to the world of zombies, demons, witches and monsters. These frightening characters are not so scary when we get to laugh at the jokes Liz Hughes has found about them.

7

What do you call an ant with five pairs of eyes? Ant-ten-eye.

What kind of ant is good at adding up? An account-ant.

What medicine do you give a sick ant? Antibiotics.

Why did the ant-elope? Nobody gnu.

What's worse than ants in your pants? A bat in your bra.

What kind of ant
can you color with?
A cray-ant.

What do you call an ant
that likes to be alone?
An independ-ant.

What do you call
an ant who can't
play the piano?
Discord-ant.

What do you call an ant
with frog's legs?
An ant-phibian.

What game do ants
play with monsters?
Squash.

How many ants are needed to fill an apartment?
Ten-ants.

Why did the elephant put his trunk across the trail?
To trip up the ants.

What is smaller than an ant's dinner?
An ant's mouth.

What is even bigger than that?
A Gi-ant.

how come they find the time to turn up at picnics?

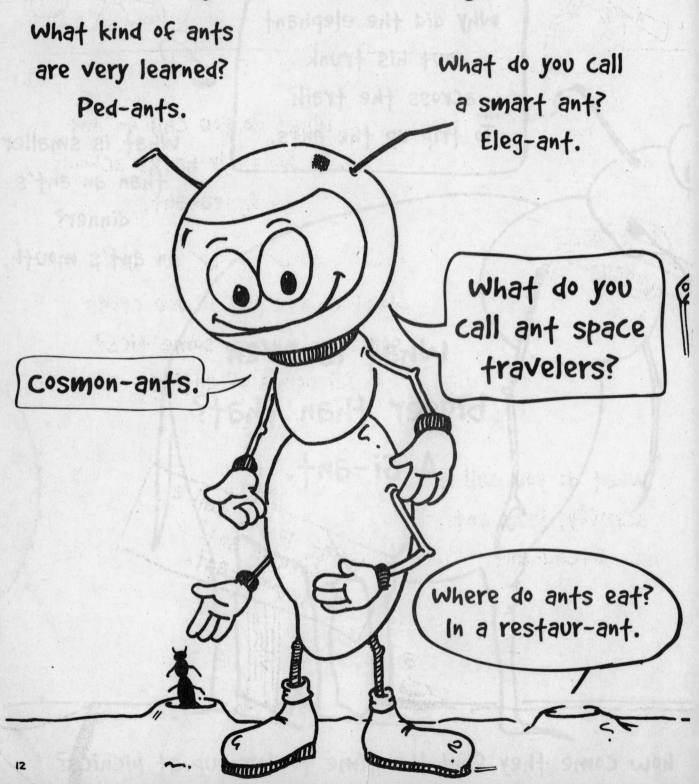

Where do ants go for their holidays?
fr-ants.

What do you call an ant who honestly hates school?
A tru-ant.

✓ ✓ ✓ ✓

What do you get if you cross some ants with some tics?
All sorts of antics.

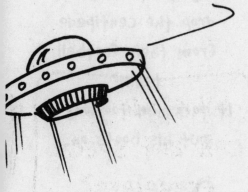

What do you call a scruffy, lazy ant?
Decad-ant.

What do you call a foreign ant?
Import-ant.

CENTIPE...

What goes 99-Clonk, 99-Clonk?
A centipede with a wooden leg.

Why did the insects
drop the centipede
from their football
team?
It took him too long to
put his boots on.

A centipede with
athlete's foot.

What do you get if
you cross
a centipede with
a parrot?
A walkie-talkie.

What's worse than a giraffe
with a sore throat?
14   A centipede with chilblains.

What has 50 legs but can't walk? Half a centipede.

What do you call a guard with 100 legs? A sentrypede.

What is worse than a crocodile with toothache?

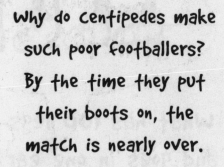

Why do centipedes make such poor footballers? By the time they put their boots on, the match is nearly over.

Why was the centipede late? Because she was playing "This Little Piggy" with her baby.

<u>Centipede to physician</u>: "Doc, when my feet hurt, I hurt all over."

© © ©

<u>Centipede to pal</u>: "I just hate it when I start the day off on the wrong foot."

What did one centipede say to another?
"You've got a lovely pair of legs, pair of legs, pair of legs..."

What has 100 legs
and goes in one ear
and out the other?
A centipede in a
corn field (geddit?).

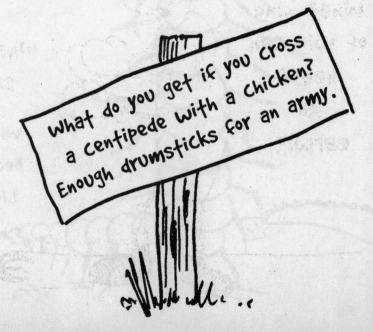

What do you get if you cross a centipede with a chicken? Enough drumsticks for an army.

EARWIGS & SPIDERS

Why don't the other insects like earwigs?
Because they're always earwigging their conversations.

What kind of wig can hear?
An earwig.

What did the earwig say when it fell down the stairs?
Ear we go!

What did Mrs Spider say to Mr Spider when he broke her new web? "Darn it!"

What do you get if you cross a tarantula with a rose? I don't know but I wouldn't try smelling one.

What happened when the chef found a daddy-long-legs in the lettuce? The insect became daddy-short-legs.

Why did the spider buy a car? He wanted to take it out for a spin.

What does a spider do when he gets angry? He goes up the wall.

What are spiders' webs good for? Spiders.

How do you know if a spider is with it? He doesn't have a web, he has a website.

What did the spiders say to the fly? "We're getting married. Do you want to come to the webbing?"

Why do spiders enjoy swimming? They have webbed feet.

What's red and dangerous? Raspberry and tarantula jelly.

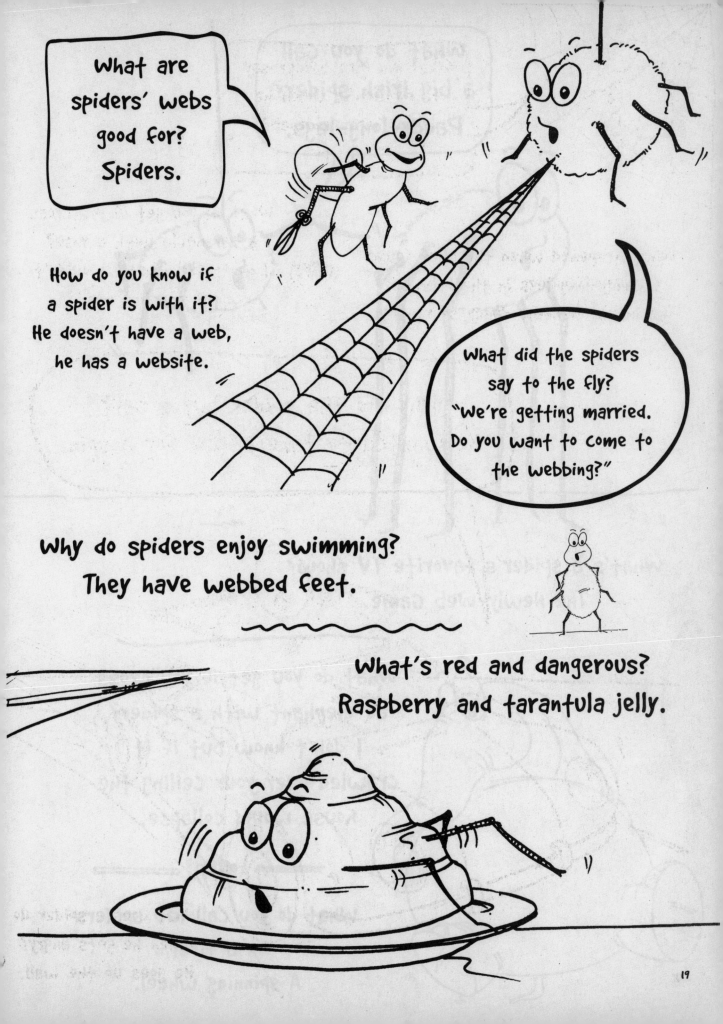

What's a spider's favorite TV show?
The Newly-web Game.

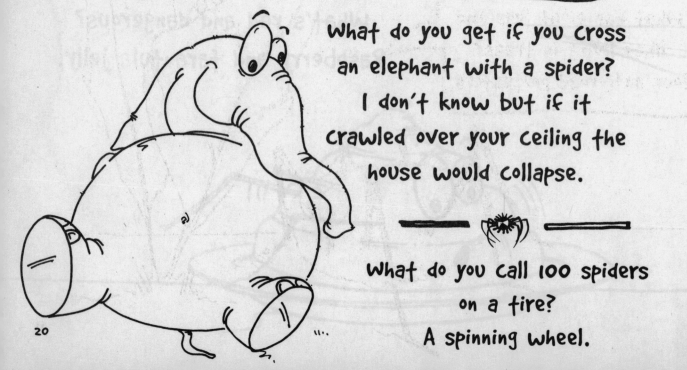

What do you get if you cross
an elephant with a spider?
I don't know but if it
crawled over your ceiling the
house would collapse.

What do you call 100 spiders
on a tire?
A spinning wheel.

What would happen if tarantulas were as big as horses?
If one bit you, you could ride it to hospital.

What did Mrs Spider say to
Mr Spider when he tried to
explain why he was late?
"You're spinning me a yarn."

What kind of doctors
are spiders like?
Spin doctors.

Why are spiders like tops?
They're always spinning.

What has eight legs and
likes living in trees?
Four anti-road protestors.

CATERPILLARS

What pillar doesn't hold a building up?

A caterpillar.

& GRASSHOPPERS

What does a cat go to sleep on?
A caterpillar.

o   o   o   o

What's green and dangerous?
A caterpillar with a hand grenade.

~~~~~~~~~~~~~~~

What does a caterpillar do on New Year's Day?
Turns over a new leaf.

~~~~~~~~~~~~

What's the definition of a caterpillar?
A worm in a fur coat.

• ▬ • ▬ • ▬ •

What has stripes and pulls a tractor?
A caterpillar tractor.

What is green and sooty and whistles when it rubs its back legs together?
Chimney cricket.

What is a grasshopper?
An insect on a pogo stick.

———————

What is green and can jump a mile a minute?
A grasshopper with hiccoughs.

———————

What do you call a grasshopper
with no legs?
A grass-hover.

Why is it better to be a
grasshopper than a cricket?
Because grasshoppers can play
cricket but there's no such game
as "Grasshopper."

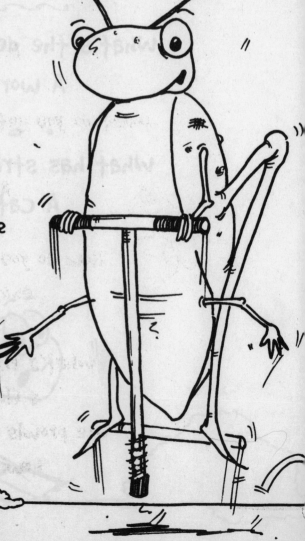

What do you call a flea that lives in an idiot's
ear?
A space invader.

✗

What do you get if you cross a flea with a
rabbit?
A bug's bunny.

○

How do you start an insect race?
one, two, flea, go!

◇

What's the difference between
a flea and a coyote?
one prowls on the hairy, the other
howls on the prairie.

What do you call a flea that lives in Russia?
A Moscow-ito.

How do you find out where a flea has bitten you?
Start from scratch.

What's the difference between fleas and dogs?
Dogs can have fleas but fleas can't have dogs.

What did the clean dog
say to the insect?
"Long time no flea!"

Who rides a dog and was a Confederate general
during the American Civil War?
Robert E. Flea.

Two fleas were running across the top of a packet of soap powder.
"Why are we running so fast?" gasped one.
"Because it says *Tear Along the Dotted Line.*"

What did one flea say to another
after a night out?
"Shall we walk home or take a dog?"

Why did the stupid boy
wear a turtle neck sweater?
To hide his flea collar.

What's a flea's favorite science fiction book?
The Itch-hiker's Guide to the Galaxy.

ITCH-HIKERS GUIDE TO THE GALAXY

What did the idiot do
to the flea in his ear?
Shot it!

What is the most faithful insect on the planet?
Fleas.
Once they find someone they like they stick to them.

What's the difference
between a flea-bitten dog
and a bored visitor?
One's going to itch.
The other's itching to go.

What insect runs away
from everything?
A flee.

What do you call a cheerful flea?
A hop-timist.

What did one amorous flea say
to the other?
"I love you aw-flea."

If a flea and a fly
pass each other,
what time is it?
fly past flea.

What's the name of
the opera about
a mouse and a flea?
Der fleadermouse.

How do fleas travel?
Itch hiking.

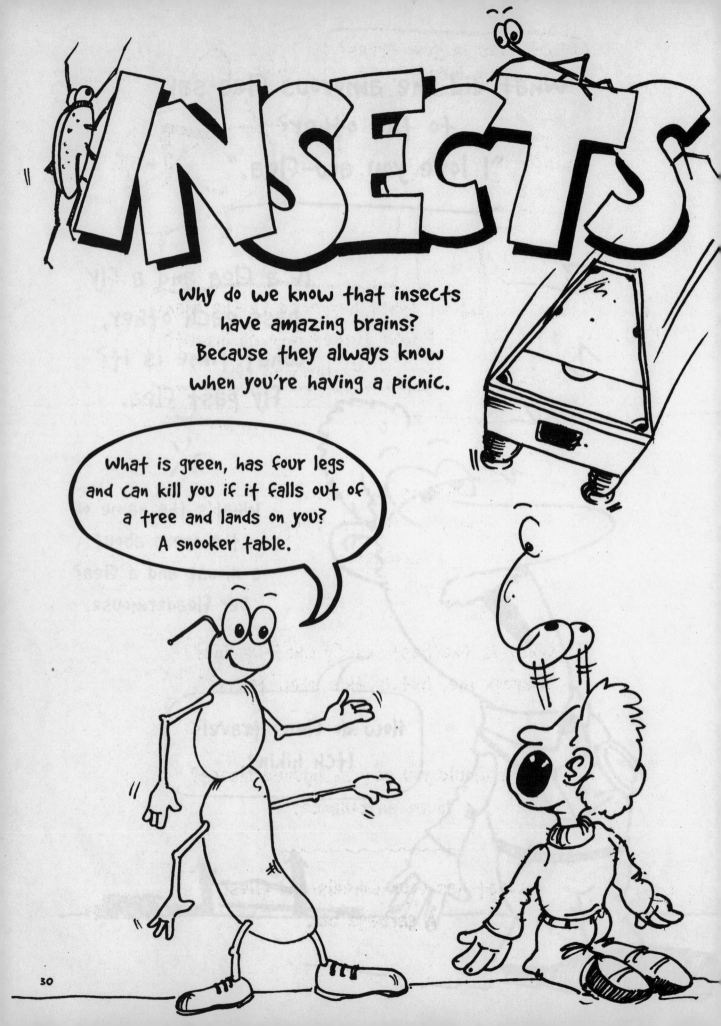

INSECTS

Why do we know that insects
have amazing brains?
Because they always know
when you're having a picnic.

What is green, has four legs
and can kill you if it falls out of
a tree and lands on you?
A snooker table.

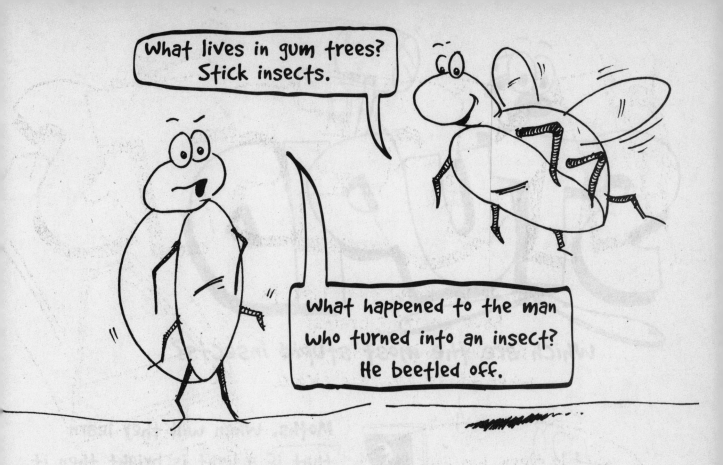

What is the insect
family's favorite game?
Cricket.

∘   ∘   ∘   ∘

What is the best insect chat-up line?
"Pardon me, but is this stool taken?"

◇   ◇   ◇   ◇

Where would you put an injured insect?
In an antbulance.

～～～～～～～～

What has four wheels and flies?
A garbage bin.

STUPID

Which are the most stupid insects?

Moths. When will they learn that if a light is bright then it probably isn't the moon? And when it's my head they're smacking into then they'll soon meet a rolled up newspaper.

Daddy Long Legs. "oh look, a human, someone far bigger than I am – I know, I'll fly into them until I've annoyed them enough to kill me, then I'll do it some more until they've completed their mission."

Bees. Shouldn't someone tell them that they'll die if they sting you?

Spiders. These are the animals that find their way into your bath, and then stay there. Why don't they get it into their heads that the bath is the last place they should explore?

Ants. So, they can carry ten times their own body weight! Thousands of years on this planet and they still haven't worked out how to build a truck!

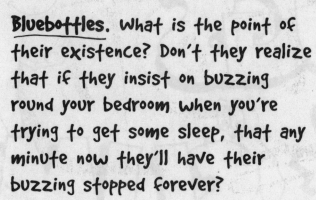

Bluebottles. What is the point of their existence? Don't they realize that if they insist on buzzing round your bedroom when you're trying to get some sleep, that any minute now they'll have their buzzing stopped forever?

Snails. Get an engine or something!

Worms. Where's the fun in spending your entire existence burrowing through muck? Get a life!

Wasps. While everyone runs a mile when they see one, why does it take hours for them to work out how to get out of a room, even after you've opened the window that they're hovering at?

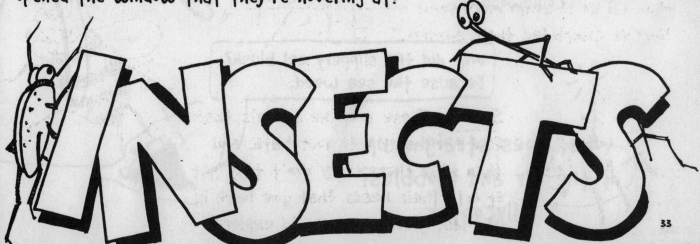

SLUGS & SLIMES

How do you start
a jellyfish race?
"Get set!"

What do you get if you cross
an octopus with a skunk?
An octopong.

What do you get if you cross a jellyfish
with a sheepdog?
Colliewobbles.

Why did the slippery eel blush?
Because the sea weed.

What goes straight up
in the air and wobbles?
A jellycopter.

What's the difference between school dinners and a pile of slugs? School dinners come on a plate.

How do you know your kitchen is filthy? The slugs leave trails on the floor that read "clean me."

What did the slug say as he slipped down the window very fast? "How slime flies!"

What did one slug say to another who had hit him and rushed off? "I'll get you next slime!"

How did the octopus lovers walk down the road? Arm in arm in arm in arm in arm in arm in arm in arm.

What was the snail doing
on the highway?
About one mile a day.

What did the octopus
say to his
moneylender?
"Here's the sick
squid I owe you."

What do octopuses play
in their spare time?
Name that tuna.

What is the
definition of a slug?
A snail with a
housing problem.

How do snails get their
shells all shiny?
They use snail varnish.

HUNGRY
&
HOMELESS

What is the strongest animal
in the world?
A snail, because it carries
its home on its back.

What gas do snails prefer?
Shell.

What do you do when two snails have a fight?
Leave them to slug it out.

What do you call a neurotic octopus?
A crazy, mixed-up squid.

What does an octopus wear when it's cold?
A coat of arms.

Where do you find giant snails?
On the ends of giants' fingers.

What do you get if you cross a bottle of water with an electric eel? A bit of a shock really!

What do you get if you cross an eel with a shopper? A slippery customer.

What did the cowboy maggot say when he went into the saloon bar? "Gimme a slug of whisky."

How did the clever snail carry his home? He used a snail-trailer.

What's slimy, tastes of raspberry,
is wobbly and lives in the sea?
A red jelly fish.

What happened when one
jelly fish met another?
They produced jelly babies.

Why did the jelly fish's
wife leave him?
He stung her into action.

What do you get if you cross
a jelly fish with an elephant?
Jelly the Elephant.

What is wobbly, slimy and
white with red spots?
A jelly fish with measles.

BUGS

What do you call a
nervous insect?
Jitterbug.

What car do insects drive?
A Volkswagen Beetle.

What do you call a top pop group made up of nits?

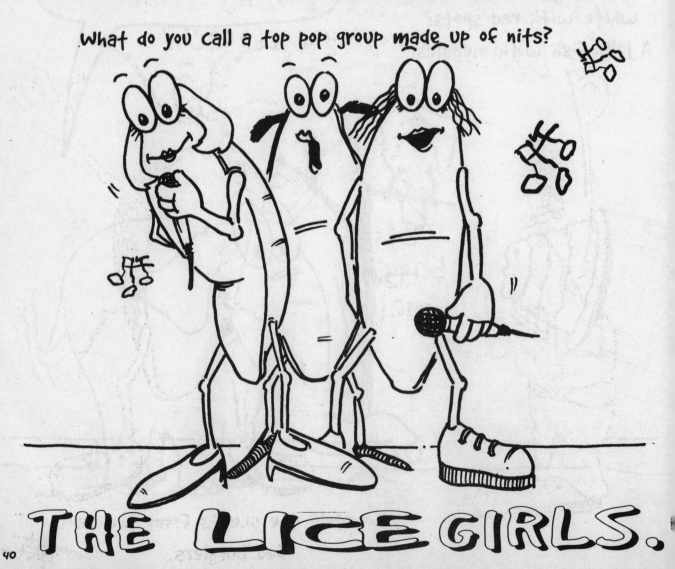

THE LICE GIRLS.

What insect can fly underwater? A bluebottle in a submarine.

What do you call an insect from outer space? Bug Rogers.

What's the grasshoppers' favorite band? Buddy Holly and the Crickets.

What do you get if you cross an elephant with some locusts? I'm not sure, but if they ever swarm - watch out!

What do you say to an annoying cockroach?

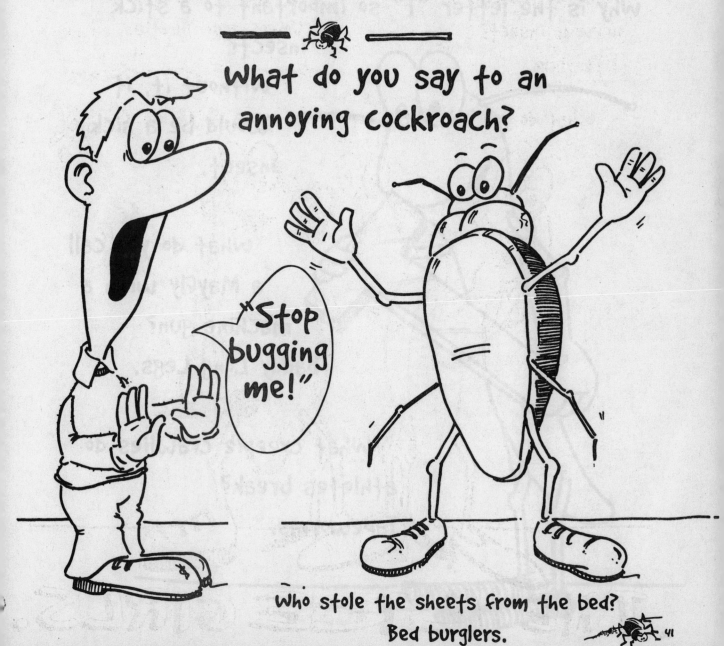

"Stop bugging me!"

Who stole the sheets from the bed? Bed burglers.

41

What do you get if you cross a praying mantis
with a termite?
A bug that says grace before eating your house.

What did one stick insect say to another?
Stick around.

Why is the letter "T" so important to a stick
insect?
Without it, it
would be a sick
insect.

What do you call
a Mayfly with a
machine gun?
Baddy Long Legs.

What creepie crawlies do
athletes break?
Tapeworms.

Why did the termite eat a sofa and two chairs?
It had a suite tooth.

How do you get rid of termites?
Exterminite them.

What lies down 100 feet in the air?
A dead centipede.

What do you call a
musical insect?
A humbug.

What kind of
insects live on
the moon?
Lunar ticks.

What's the difference
between head lice and
nits?
A nit is too stupid to
find your head.

43

What's the difference between a maggot and a cockroach?
cockroaches crunch more when you eat them.

How do insects
travel when they
go on holiday?
They go for a buggy
ride.

Why was
the insect kicked out of the park?
It was a litterbug.

What is the insect's
favorite pop group?
The Beatles.

What do you call
singing insects?
Humbugs.

What did one insect say to the other?
Stop bugging me.

What is a termite's favorite
breakfast?
Oak-meal.

What did one termite say to the other
termite when he saw a house burning?
Barbecue tonight!

What do you call an amorous insect?
The Love Bug.

What do you call an insect that has
just flown by?
A flu bug.

What did the termite say in
the pub?
"Is the bar tender here?"

What did the termite
say when he saw
that his friends
had eaten a chair?
"Wooden you know it!"

How do you keep flies out of the kitchen?
Put a bucket of manure in the lounge.

What's the difference between a fly and a bird?
A bird can fly but a fly can't bird.

Why did the fly fly?
Because the spider spied 'er.

Why did the firefly keep stealing things?
He was light-fingered.

— 🐞 —

What goes "snap, crackle, pop"?
A firefly with a short circuit.

— 🐞 —

Which fly makes films?

Stephen Spielbug.

How do fireflies start a race?
"Ready, steady, glow!"

What did one firefly say to another?
"Got to glow now."

Time flies like an arrow, but fruit flies like a banana.

Why were the flies playing football in a saucer?

They were playing for the cup.

A little firefly was in school one day and he put up his
hand. "Please miss, may I be excused?"
"Yes," replied the teacher, "when you've got to glow,
you've got to glow."

✗   ✗   ✗   ✗

If there are five flies in the kitchen, which one is the
American football player?
The one in the sugar bowl.

MOSQUI

What do you get if you cross the Lone Ranger with an insect? The Masked-quito.

What has antlers and sucks your blood? A moose-quito.

Why did the mosquito go to the dentist? To improve his bite.

What is a mosquito's favorite sport? Skin-diving.

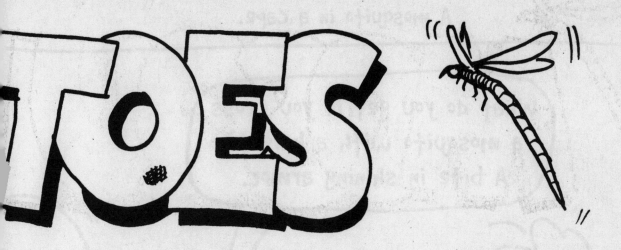

TOES

How do you know if you have a tough mosquito?
If you slap him, he slaps you back.

What's the difference between a mosquito and a fly?
Try sewing buttons on a mosquito!

What's the difference between a lawyer and a mosquito?
A mosquito drops off you when you die.

Why is it best to be bitten quickly by one mosquito?
Because an itch in time saves nine.

Which is the most religious
insect in the Middle East?
A mosque-ito.

What has six legs, bites
and talks in code?
A morse-quito.

What wears a black cape, flies through the night and sucks blood?
A mosquito in a cape.

What's the mosquitoes'
favorite song?
I've Got You Under My Skin.

What do you call "A Tale
of Two Mosquitoes"?
A bite-time story.

Why are mosquitoes
religious?
They prey on you.

What did one mosquito say
to another when they came
out of the cinema?
"Fancy a bite?"

What is small, gray, sucks
blood and eats cheese?
A mouse-quito.

WIGGLIES

What did one maggot say to
his friend stuck in an apple?
"Worm your way out of that one, then!"

Why didn't the two worms go into
Noah's ark in an apple?
Because everyone had to go in pairs.

What's worse than finding
a maggot in your apple?
Finding half a maggot
in your apple.

How can you tell which end
of a worm is its head?
Tickle its middle and see
which end smiles.

How do you make
a glow worm happy?
Cut off its tail.
It'll be de-lighted.

What is the glow-worms' favorite song?
Wake Me Up Before You Glow Glow by Wham!

Why was the glow-worm unhappy?
Because her children were not very bright.

What do you get
if you cross a
glow-worm with
a pint of beer?
Light ale.

What do you get if you cross
a worm with a young goat?
A dirty kid.

What do worms
leave round their
bathtubs?
The scum of
the earth.

How can you tell if you are looking at a police glow-worm?
He has a blue light.

What is the worms' favorite band?

Who is the worms' Prime Minister?

Mud.

Maggot Thatcher.

What happened to the glow-worm who was squashed? He was de-lighted.

◇

What's the maggot army called? The Apple corps.

◇

What is the best advice to give a worm? Sleep late.

When should you stop for a glow-worm?

When he has a red light.

What's the difference between a worm and a gooseberry?
Ever tried eating worm pie?

What do you get if you cross a worm with an elephant?
Big holes in your garden.

What did one worm say to another when he was late home?

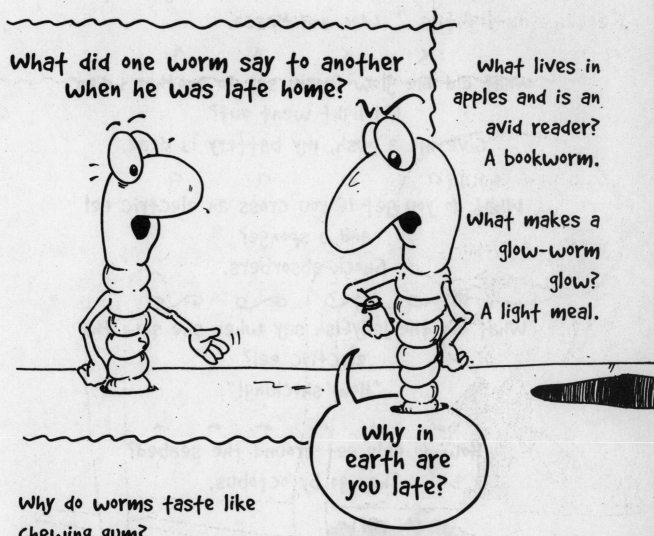

Why in earth are you late?

What lives in apples and is an avid reader?
A bookworm.

What makes a glow-worm glow?
A light meal.

Why do worms taste like chewing gum?
Because they're Wrigley's.

One woodworm met another.
"How's life?" she asked. "Oh, same as usual," he replied, "boring."

Why did the sparrow fly into the library?
It was looking for bookworms.

What would you do if you found a bookworm
chewing your favorite book?
Take the words right out of its mouth.

What is a bookworm's idea of a big feast?
War and Peace.

What did one glow-worm say to another when
his light went out?
"Give me a push, my battery is dead."

What do you get if you cross an electric eel
and a sponge?
Shock absorbers.

What did the jellyfish say when she saw the
electric eel?
"How shocking!"

How do eels get around the seabed?
They go by octobus.

Who was wet and slippery and invaded England?
William the conger.

What is wet and slippery and
likes Latin American music?

A conga
eel.

What's wet and wiggly and says how do you do 16 times?
Two octopuses shaking hands.

What is an eel's favorite song?
Slip Sliding Away.

MOTHS & BUTTERFLIES

What do insects learn at school?
Mothematics.

How do you make a butterfly?
Flick it out of the dish with a butter knife.

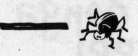

What insect lives on nothing?
A moth, because it eats holes.

What is pretty and delicate and carries a sub-machine gun?
A killer butterfly.

How can you make a moth ball?
Hit it with a fly-swatter.

What do you get if you cross a moth with a firefly? An insect that can find its way around a dark wardrobe.

How do stones stop moths eating your clothes? Because rolling stones gather no moths.

What is a myth? A female moth.

Who do all moths bow to? The Moth-er Superior.

Why did the moth nibble a hole in the carpet? He wanted to see the floor show.

Why was the moth so unpopular?
He kept picking holes in everything.

· · · · · · ·

What likes to spend the
summer in a fur coat
and the winter in a
swim-suit?

A moth.

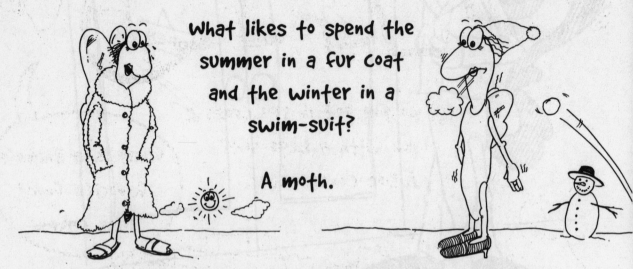

Why wouldn't they let the butterfly into the dance?
Because it was a moth ball.

~~~~~~~~~~

Why did the butterfly?
Because it saw the milk-float.

· · · · · ·

What circles the lampshade
at 200 mph?

Stirling Moth.

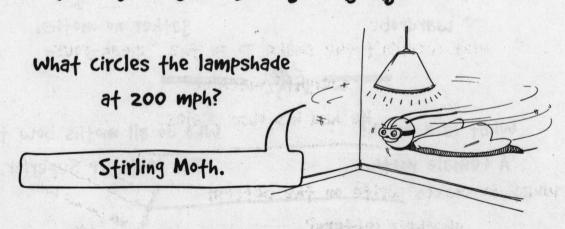

Which is the biggest moth in the world?
A mammoth.

SNAKES

What do you get if you cross a
snake with a Lego set?
A boa constructor.

What is a snake's
favorite food?
Hiss cakes.

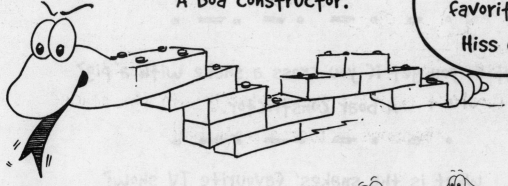

Why do babies like cobras?
Because they come with their
own rattle.

Why wouldn't the snake go on the "speak-your-
weight" machine?
He had his own scales.

What do snakes write on the bottom
of their letters?
"With love and hisses."

With love and hisses,
Cobra

How can you tell if a snake is a baby?
It has a rattle.

• ▫ ▬ • ▬ • ▬ • ▫ ▬ •

What did the snake say when he was offered a piece
of cheese for dinner?
"Thank you, I'll just have a slither."

• ▫ ▬ • ▬ • ▫ ▬ • ▫ ▬ •

What's another word for a python?
A mega-bite.

• ▫ ▬ • ▬ • ▫ ▬ • ▫ ▬ •

What do you get if you cross a snake with a pig?
A boar constrictor.

• ▫ ▬ • ▬ ▬ • ▬ • ▫ ▬ •

What is the snakes' favourite TV show?
Monty Python.

What snakes are good at sums?
Adders.

Which hand would you use to grab a poisonous snake?
Someone else's.

What do you do if you find a black mamba in your toilet?
Wait until he's finished.

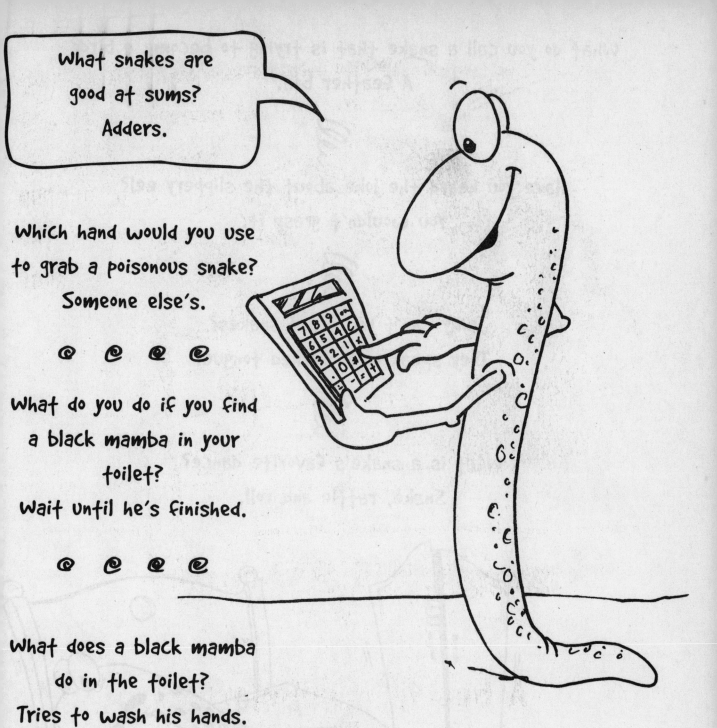

What does a black mamba do in the toilet?
Tries to wash his hands.

What is a snake's favorite opera?
Wriggletto.

What do you get if you cross a serpent and a trumpet?
A snake in the brass.

What do you call a snake that is trying to become a bird?
A feather boa.

Have you heard the joke about the slippery eel?
You wouldn't grasp it.

Why can't you trust snakes?
They speak with forked tongue.

What is a snake's favorite dance?
Snake, rattle and roll.

What should you do if you
find a snake in your bed?
Sleep in the wardrobe.

What do you get if you cross a snake
with a hotdog?
A fangfurther.

What's the snake's second
favorite dance?
The mamba.

What did one snake say to another?
Hiss off!

Why did the two boa constrictors
get married?
Because they had a crush on each other.

What is the difference between a poisonous snake
and a headmaster?
You can make a pet out of the snake.

69

What kind of snake is useful on your windscreen?

A viper.

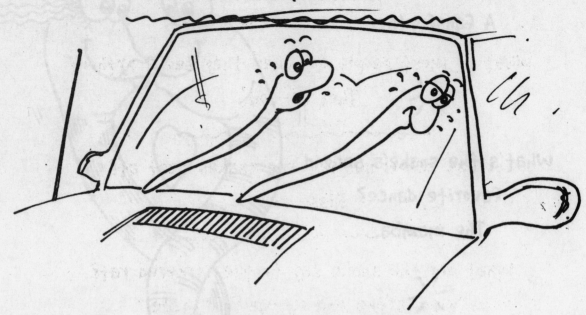

Why are snakes hard to fool?

They have no leg to pull.

What is the python's favorite pop group?

Squeeze.

What perfume do lady snakes like to wear?

Poison by Dior.

What do you get if you cross a bag of snakes with a cupboard of food?

Snakes and Larders.

Why did the viper want to become a python?

He got the coiling.

What do you call a python with a great bedside manner?
A snake charmer.

~~~~~~~~~~~~~~~~~~

What do most people do when they see a python?
They re-coil.

~~~~~~~~~~~~~~~~~~

What school subject are snakes best at?
Hiss-tory.

~~~~~~~~~~~~~~~~~~

What did the snake say to the cornered rat?
"Hiss is the end of the line mate!"

71

What do snakes have on their bath towels?
"Hiss and Hers."

What do you call a snake that informs the police?
A grass-snake.

What did the python say to the viper?
"I've got a crush on you."

What do you get if you cross two snakes with a magic spell?
Addercadabra and abradacobra.

What did the mummy snake say to her crying baby?
"Stop crying and viper your nose."

What's the best thing about deadly snakes?
They've got poisonality.

Why did the python do National Service?
He was coiled up.

What's a python's favorite flower?
Coily-flowers.

What song do snakes like to sing?
"Viva Aspana."

What happened when a deadly rattlesnake bit a witch?
He died in agony.

↑ ✗ ✗ ✗

Why did the viper, viper nose?
Because the adder adder handkerchief.

↑ ✗ ✗

What did one snake say when the other snake asked him the time?
"Don't asp me!"

↑ ✗ ✗ ✗

What do you give a sick snake?
Asp-rin.

✗ ✗ ✗

What do you call a snake who works for the government?
A civil serpent.

What do baby pythons play with?
Rattle-snakes.

What kind of letters did the snake get from his admirers?
Fang mail.

What's long and green and goes hith?
A snake with a lisp.

"So glad to meet you," said the Hindu politely.
"Charmed I'm sure," replied the snake.

Why did some snakes disobey Noah when he told
them to "go forth and multiply"?
They couldn't - they were adders.

What would you get if you crossed a new-born snake
with a basket-ball?
A bouncing baby boa.

Which snakes are found on cars?
Windscreen vipers.

What powerful reptile
is found in the Sydney
opera House?
The Lizard of oz.

What's the definition
of a nervous
breakdown?
A chameleon on a
tartan rug.

How do frogs manage to lay so many eggs?
They sit eggsaminations.

What kind of tiles can't you stick on the wall?
Rep-tiles.

What do you call a rich frog?
A gold-blooded reptile.

What do headmasters and bullfrogs have in common?
Both have a big head that consists mostly of mouth.

What kind of bull doesn't have horns?
A bullfrog.

What jumps up and down in front of a car?
Froglights.

Where do frogs keep their money?
In a river bank.

What happened to the lizard in the wizard's garden pond?
He had him newt-ered.

What did one frog say to the other?
"Time's sure fun when you're having flies!"

What happened when
the frog joined the
cricket team?
He bowled long hops.

Why did the toad
become a lighthouse
keeper?
He had his own
frog-horn.

What did the bus conductor say to the frog?
"Hop on."

What do you say to a hitch-hiking frog?
"Hop in!"

What do you get if you cross a frog with a ferry?
A hoppercraft.

What do you call a frog who wants to be a cowboy?
Hoppalong Cassidy.

When is a car like a frog?
When it's being toad.

Why do frogs have webbed feet?
To stamp out forest fires.

~~~~~~~

What do you say if you meet a toad?
Wart's new?

~~~~~~~

What's green and can jump a mile a minute?
A frog with hiccoughs.

~~~~~~~

Why did the lizard go on a diet?
It weighed too much for its scales.

~~~~~~~

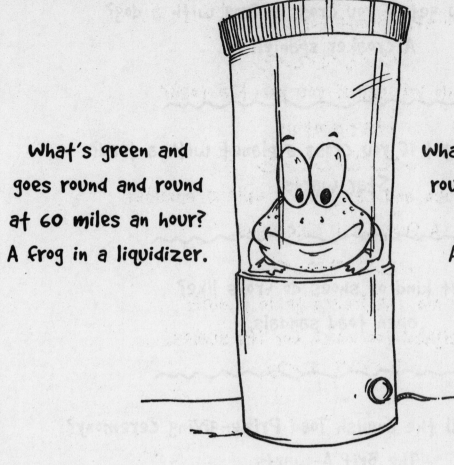

What's green and goes round and round at 60 miles an hour? A frog in a liquidizer.

What is yellow and goes round and round at 60 miles an hour? A mouldy frog in a liquidizer.

Why was the frog down-in-the-mouth?
He was un-hoppy.

How do frogs die?
They Kermit suicide.

What is a frog's favorite flower?
The croakus.

What is a frog's favorite game?
Croak-et.

What do you get if you cross a frog with a dog?
A croaker spaniel.

What do you get if you cross a planet with a toad?
Star warts.

What kind of shoes do frogs like?
Open toad sandals.

What do you call the English Toad Prize-giving ceremony?
The Brit A-warts.

Why doesn't Kermit like elephants? They always want to play leap-frog with him.

Why is a frog luckier than a cat?

Because a frog croaks all the time - a cat only croaks nine times.

What is a toad's favorite ballet?
Swamp lake.

What do toads drink?
croaka-cola.

What do frogs drink?
Hot croako.

What is green and slimy and is found at the North Pole?
A lost frog.

Where do frogs keep their treasure?
In a croak of gold at the end of the rainbow.

✗   ✗   ✗

What do you call an 80-year-old frog?
An old croak.

✗   ✗

What do you get if you cross a toad with mist?
Kermit the fog.

✗   ✗

What is a toad's favorite sweet?
Lollihops.

What do you call a
frog spy?
A croak and dagger
agent.

What do
you call a
girl with a
frog on her
head?
Lily.

What do Scottish toads play?

Hop-scotch.

How did the toad die?

It simply croaked.

What goes dot-dot-croak, dot-dot-croak?

Morse toad.

What's the weakest animal in the world?

A toad. He will croak if you touch him.

What's white on the outside, green on the inside and comes with relish and onions?

A hot frog.

What happens if you eat a hot-frog?

You croak in no time.

Where do toads leave their coats and hats?

In the croakroom.

What is green and tough?
A toad with a machine gun.

What is the chameleon's motto?
A change is as good as a rest.

~~~~~~~~~~~~~~~~~~~~~~~~~~~~~~

Why did the tadpole feel lonely?
Because he was newt to the area.

~~~~~~~~~~~~~~~~~~~~~~~~~~~~~~

What kind of pole is short and floppy?
A tadpole.

~~~~~~~~~~~~~~~~~~~~~~~~~~~~~~

Where do you get frogs eggs?
In a spawn shop.

~~~~~~~~~~~~~~~~~~~~~~~~~~~~~~

Why didn't the famale frog lay eggs?
Because her husband spawned her affections.

RODENTS

What is the definition of a narrow
squeak?
A thin mouse.

What goes "eek, eek, bang"?
A mouse in a minefield.

What's gray and squeaky and hangs
around in caves?
Stalagmice.

Which mouse was a Roman emperor?
Julius Cheeser.

Who is the king of all the mice?
Mouse Tse Tung.

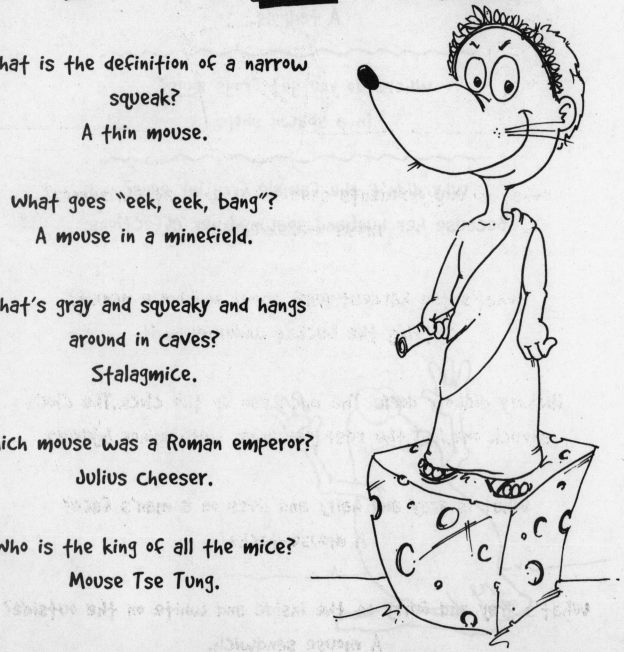

What do angry rodents send each other at Christmas?
Cross mouse Cards.

What's the hardest part about milking a mouse?
Getting the bucket underneath it.

Hickory dickory dock. The mice ran up the clock. The clock
struck one, And the rest got away with minor injuries.

What is gray and hairy and lives on a man's face?
A mouse-tache.

What's gray and furry on the inside and white on the outside?
A mouse sandwich.

What do you call a mouse that can
pick up a monster?
Sir.

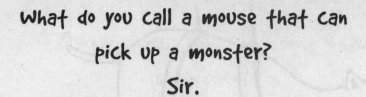

How do mice celebrate when they move house?
With a mouse-warming party.

What did the mouse say when his friend broke his
front teeth?
Hard cheese.

What is a mouse's favorite game?
Hide and squeak.

Why did the mouse eat a candle?
For light refreshment.

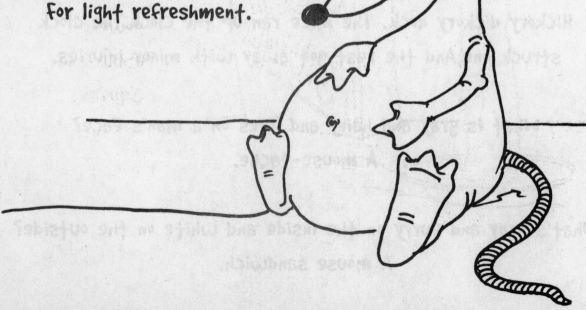

What goes "dot, dot, dash, squeak"?
Mouse code.

Who has large antlers, a high voice and wears white gloves?
Mickey Moose.

What is small, furry and smells like bacon?
A hamster.

What do you get if you cross a mouse with a packet of soap powder?
Bubble and Squeak.

What is a mouse's favorite record?
Please cheese me.

How do you save a drowning rodent?
Use mouse to mouse resuscitation.

What kind of musical instrument do rats play?
Mouse organ.

Why do mice need oiling?
Because they squeak.

What do confused owls say?

"Too-whit-to-why?"

OWLS

What do two lovesick owls say when it's raining?
"Too-wet-to-woo!"

What sits in a tree and says "Hoots mon, hoots mon"?
A Scottish owl.

Why were the mummy and daddy owls worried about their son?
Because he didn't seem to give a hoot anymore.

What did the owl say to his friend as he flew off?
"Owl be seeing you later."

Why did the owl, 'owl?
Because the woodpecker would peck 'er.

What did the baby owl's parents say when he
wanted to go to a party?
"You're not owld enough."

What did the owls do when one of them had a punk haircut?
They hooted with laughter.

What do Scottish owls sing?   What did the scornful owl say?
Owld Lang Sine.   "Twit twoo."

How do you know that owls are cleverer than chickens?
Have you ever heard of Kentucky fried owl?

What do bees do if they want to use public transport?

Wait at a buzz stop.

What do you get if you cross a bee with a skunk?
A creature that stinks and stings.

What does a queen bee do when she belches?
She issues a royal pardon.

How does a queen bee get around the hive?
She's throne.

What's yellow and brown and covered in blackberries?
A bramble bee.

What is more dangerous than being with a fool?
Fooling with a bee.

Why did the bee start spouting poetry?
He was waxing lyrical.

Who is the bees' favorite composer?
Bee-thoven.

Who wrote books for little bees?
Bee-trix Potter.

What did the mummy bee say to the
naughty little bee?

"Bee-hive
yourself!"

What goes "hum-choo, hum-choo"?
A bee with a cold.

What is a bee-line?
The shortest distance between two buzz-stops.

What's the difference between a very old,
shaggy Yeti and a dead bee?
one's a seedy beast and the other's a deceased bee.

What do you call a bee who's had a spell put on him?
Bee-witched.

Can bees fly in the rain?
Not without their little yellow jackets.

What has brown and yellow stripes and buzzes along at the bottom of the sea?

A bee in a submarine.

Why do bees hum?
Because they've forgotten the words.

What kind of bee hums and drops things?
A fumble bee.

What did the bee say to the flower?
"Hello honey."

What are the bees' favorite flowers?
Bee-gonias.

What is brown and yellow and buzzes at 36,000 feet?
A bee in an aeroplane.

What did the confused bee say?
"To bee or not to bee."

What are the cleverest bees?
Spelling bees.

Which bee is good for your health?
Vitamin bee.

What goes zzub, zzub?
A bee flying backwards.

Why do bees buzz?
They can't whistle.

What do you call a bee born in May?
A maybe.

What bee can never be understood?
A mumble-bee.

What do you get if you cross a bee with a quarter of a pound of mince?
A humburger.

Who is a bee's favorite painter?

Pablo Beecasso.

What did the spider say to the bee?

"Your honey or your life."

What is a baby bee?
A little humbug.

What is the bees' favorite film?
The Sting.

Who's top of the pops in the beehive?
Sting.

What did the drone say to the Queen Bee?
"Swarm in here isn't it?"

Where do bees keep their money?
In a honey-box.

—————

Which is the bees' favorite pop group?
The Bee Gees.

—————

What is the bees' favorite TV channel?
The Bee Bee C.

—————

What is the bees' favorite novel?
The Great Gats-bee.

—————

What do you get if you cross a bee
with a door-bell?
A hum-dinger.

How many bees do you need in a proper bee choir?
A humdred.

— o — . o . — . o .

What does the bee Santa Claus say at Christmas?

Ho-hum-hum.

Why did the bees go on strike?
Because they wanted more honey and shorter working flowers.

Why do bees have sticky hair?
Because of the honey combs.

Where do bees come from?
Stingapore.

What kind of gum do bees chew?
Bumble-gum.

Why did the queen bee kick all the other bees out of the hive?
Because they kept droning on and on.

What does a bee say before it stings you?
"This is going to hurt me much more than it hurts you."

What do you call a bee that can shelter a plane?
An aero-drone.

If bees make honey what do wasps make?

waspberry jam.

Where do you take a sick wasp?
To waspital.

What is the wasps' favorite song?
"Just a Spoonful of Sugar."

What did the bee say to the wasp as he
tried to make honey?
"Don't wasp your time!"

The Fly

Batman

Beetlejuice

The Sting

The Good, the Bug and the Ugly

Spawn

The Frog Prince

Four Webbings and a Funeral

Seven Bats for Seven Brothers

Shall we have a lice-cream?

What insects watch at the cinema.

Why did the bat miss the bus?

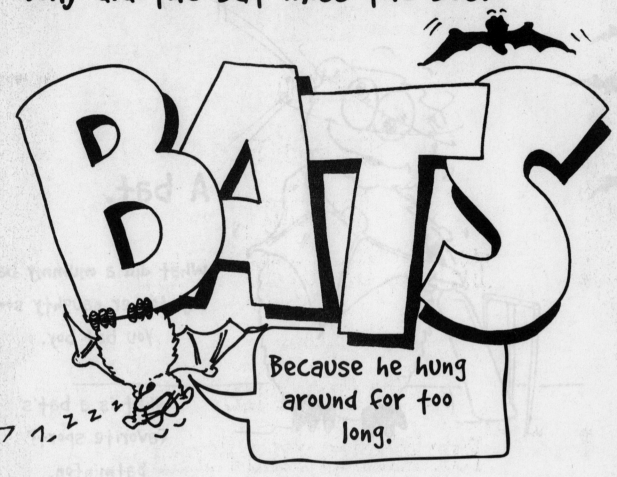

BATS

Because he hung around for too long.

What did the bat pop group call themselves?
The Boom Town Bats.

What did one bat say to another?
"Let's hang around together."

What did The Terminator say to Batman?
"I'll be bat!"

What animal is the most use at a cricket match?

A bat.

What did a mummy bat say to her naughty son? You bat boy.

What is a bat's favorite sport? Batminton.

Who is the bat's favorite hero? Batman of course!

Why don't bats get kissed much? They have bat breath.

What would you get if you crossed a bat with a magician? A flying sorcerer.

What is the best way to hold a bat? By its handle.

What do bats do at night?
Aerobatics.

What do you get if you cross a
bat with a Womble?
A wombat.

What do you
call a bat in a
bellfry?
A dingbat.

What is the first thing that bats
learn at school?
The alphabat.

What do you call a little bat?
A battle.

What do bats sing
when
it's raining?

"Raindrops keep
falling on my
feet."

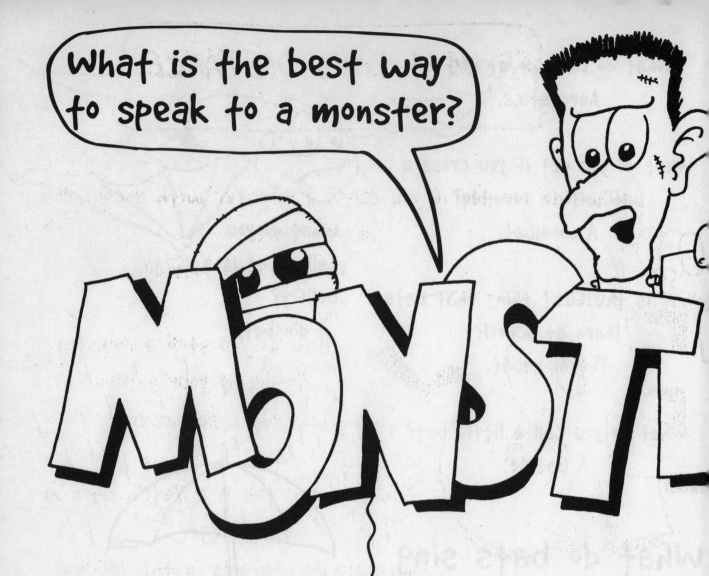

What is the best way to speak to a monster?

What does a polite monster say when he meets you for the first time?
"Pleased to eat you!"

How do you tell a good monster from a bad one?
If it's a good one you will be able to talk about it later!

Why did the monster-breeder call his monster "fog"?
Because he was gray and thick.

Why did the monster visit the psychiatrist?
Because he thought everyone was beginning to love him.

110

what do you get if you cross a m...
an oat fie...
Mega l...

what do you

How do you stop a monster
digging up your garden?
Take his spade away.

How can you tell if a Yeti's been in
the fridge?
There are paw-prints in the trifle.

What do you call a monster with a wooden head?
Edward.

What do you call a monster with two wooden heads?
Edward Woodward.

What do you call a monster with four wooden heads?
I don't know but Edward Woodward would.

...get if you cross King Kong with a snowman? Frostbite.

What do you do with a blue monster? Try and cheer him up.

Why did the two cyclops fight? They could never see eye to eye over anything.

What is as big as King Kong but doesn't weigh anything? King Kong's shadow.

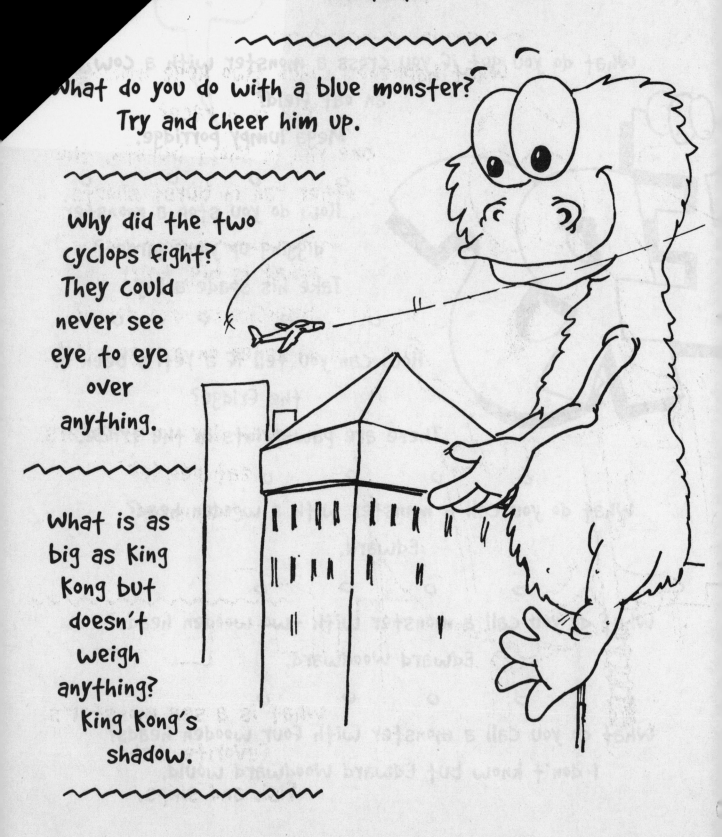

What kind of money do yetis use?
Iced lolly.

What happened when two huge monsters
ran in a race?
One ran in short bursts, the
other ran in burst shorts.

What is big, hairy and
bounces up and down?
A monster on a pogo stick.

On which day do monsters
eat people?
Chewsday.

What is a sea monster's
favorite dish?
Fish and ships.

What followed the Loch Ness monster?

A whopping big tail.

What's blue and hairy and goes round and round?
A monster on a turntable.

What do you get if you cross King Kong with a watchdog?
A terrified postman.

What's yellow, brown and hairy?
Cheese on toast dropped on the carpet.

What's the difference between Frankenstein and boiled potatoes?
You can't mash Frankenstein.

What do you do with a green monster?
Put it in the sun until it ripens!

What's brown and furry on the inside and clear on the outside?
King Kong in clingfilm.

What did the Loch Ness monster say to his friend?
Long time no sea.

What kind of monster can sit on the end of your finger?
The bogeyman.

Can the Abominable Snowman jump very high?
Hardly - he can only just clear his throat!

Why did King Kong paint the bottoms of his feet brown?
So that he could hide upside down in a jar of peanut butter.

What do you get if you cross a giant, hairy monster with a penguin?
I don't know but it's a very tight-fitting dinner suit.

What do you get if you cross a long-fanged, purple-spotted monster with a cat?

What can a monster do that you can't?
Count up to 25 on his fingers.

Why didn't King Kong go to Hong Kong?
He didn't like Chinese food.

What kind of cocktails do monsters enjoy?
'Ighballs.

What does a monster mum say to her kids at dinnertime?
"Don't talk with someone in your mouth."

What did the monster want to eat in the restaurant?
The finger bowl.

Which is the most dangerous animal in the northern hemisphere?
Yak the Ripper.

A town that is free of dogs.

What is big, hairy and can fly faster than sound.
King Koncord.

Why did the monster cross the road?
He wanted to know what it was like to be a
chicken.

Why is King Kong big and hairy?
So you can tell him apart from a gooseberry.

How can you tell the difference between a rabbit
and a red-eyed monster?
Just try getting a red-eyed monster into a rabbit
hutch.

How do you catch King Kong?
Hang upside down and make a noise like a banana.

What do you give a monster with big feet?
Big flippers.

What do you get if you cross King Kong with a budgie?
A messy cage.

How do you know if a monster's come round for tea?
There are muddy footprints on the carpet.

What time is it when a monster sits on your garden wall?
Time to mend the garden wall.

Two purple, hairy monsters were walking along the seafront and one said to the other, "It's quiet for a Bank Holiday Monday."

How do you know when there's a monster under your bed?

Why did the monster paint himself in rainbow colors?
Because he wanted to hide in the crayon box.

What do you give a seasick yeti?
Plenty of room.

What do monsters play when they are in the bus?
Squash.

How do you get six monsters in a biscuit tin?
Take the biscuits out first.

Your nose touches the ceiling.

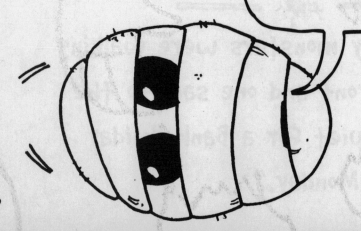

120

Where are yetis found?
They're so big they're hardly
ever lost.

What's big, heavy, furry,
dangerous and has 16
wheels?
A monster on roller-
skates.

Why did the monster
have green ears and a
red nose?
So that he could hide in
rhubarb patches.

What do you
get if
King Kong
sits on
your worst
enemy?
A flatworm.

What's the difference between a monster and a fly?

Quite a lot really.

What do you get if King Kong sits on your piano?
A flat note.

Why shouldn't you dance with a yeti?
Because if it trod on you, you might get flat feet.

How do you get a monster into a mini.
open the door.

What do you call a yeti in a phone box?
Stuck.

What do you call a Scottish sea monster who hangs people?
The Loch Noose Monster

How did the yeti feel when he
had flu?
Abominable.

What do you get if you cross a
fashion designer with a sea
monster?
The Loch Dress Monster.

Who won the Monster Beauty
contest?
No one.

What happened when the nasty
monster stole a pig?
The pig squealed to the police.

What happened when the
stupid monster went
shoplifting?
He stole a free sample.

MONSTER
BEAUTY CONTEST

What happened when the big, black monster became a chimney sweep?
He started a grime wave.

What do nasty monsters give each other for breakfast?
Smacks in the mouth.

What do you call a huge, ugly, slobbering, furry monster with cotton wool in his ears?
Anything you like – he can't hear you.

How do you know if a monster is musical?
He's got a flat head.

What do you call a mammoth who conducts an orchestra?
Tuskanini.

What's the hardest part of
making monster soup?
Stirring it.

How does frankenstein sit
in his Chair?
Bolt upright.

What aftershave do
monsters wear?
Brute.

What did one of frankenstein's
ears say to the other?
"I didn't know we lived on the
same block."

How can you tell if a monster has a glass eye?
Because it comes out in conversation.

◇   ◇   ◇   ◇

What did one of the monster's eyes say to the other?
"Between us is something that smells."

If King Kong came to England why would he live in the
Tower of London?
Because he's a beef-eater.

◇   ◇   ◇

What do yetis eat on top
of Everest?
High Tea.

Why was the big,
hairy, two-headed
monster top of the
class at school?

Because two heads
are better than
one.

What happens if a big, hairy monster sits in
front of you at the cinema?
You miss most of the film.

◇ ◇ ◇ ◇

What happened when a purple-headed monster took up singing?
He had a frog in his throat.

━ ━ ━ ━

What did the monster say when he ate Aesop?
"Make a fable out of that then!"

◇ ◇ ◇ ◇

What should you do if you are on a picnic with King Kong?
Give him the biggest bananas.

Who brings monsters' babies?
Frankenstork.

◇   ◇   ◇

How do you know that there's a monster
in your bath?
You can't get the shower curtain closed.

◇   ◇   ◇   ◇

Why couldn't Swamp Thing go to the party?
Because he was bogged down in his work.

◇

What's the height of impossibility?
The Abominable Snowman trying to get a suntan.

What happened when the monster fell down a well?
He kicked the bucket.

Why was the Abominable Snowman's dog called Frost?
Because Frost bites.

How do you greet a three-headed monster?
Hello, hello, hello.

Why was the monster standing on his head?
He was turning things over in his mind.

How did the world's tallest monster become short overnight?
Someone stole all his money.

・ ▭ ・ ▬ ・ ▭ ・ ▭ ・

What kind of man doesn't like to sit in front of the fire?
An Abominable Snowman.

・ ▭ ・ ▭ ▬ ・ ▬ ・ ▭ ・

How do Abominable Snowmen feel when they melt?
Abominable!

・ ▭ ・ ▬ ・ ▭ ・ ▭ ・

What do Abominable Snowmen call their offspring?
Chill-dren.

・ ▭ ・ ▬ ・ ▭ ・ ▭ ・ ▭ ・

What did the big, hairy monster do when he lost a hand?
He went to the secondhand shop.

・ ▭ ・ ▬ ・ ▭ ・ ▭ ・ ▭ ・

Where do Abominable Snowmen go to dance?
To snowballs.

・ ▭ ・ ▭ ・ ▭ ・ ▭ ・ ▭ ・

Why did the fat, hairy, drooling monster stop going out in the sunshine?
He didn't want to spoil his looks.

What did one Abominable Snowman say to the other?
"I'm afraid I just don't believe in people."

What is the Abominable Snowman's favorite book?
War and Frozen Peas.

What did the Abominable Snowman do after he had had his teeth pulled out?
He ate the dentist.

Why did the Abominable Snowman send his father to Siberia?
Because he wanted frozen pop.

Why did the monster dye his hair yellow?
He wanted to see if blonds have more fun.

How does a yeti get to work?
By icicle.

What does a yeti eat for dinner?
Ice-burgers.

What happened when the monster stole a
bottle of perfume?
He was convicted of fragrancy.

Why did King Kong join the army?
He wanted to know about gorilla warfare.

What should you do if a monster runs
through your front door?
Run through the back door.

What do you get if you cross King Kong with a frog?

A gorilla that catches aeroplanes with its tongue.

What business is King Kong in?

Monkey business.

Who is the smelliest, hairiest monarch in the world?

King Pong.

What would you get if you crossed King Kong
with a skunk?

I don't know but it could always get
a seat on a bus!

Why do monsters have lots of
matted fur?

Because they'd look silly in plastic raincoats.

Where does King Kong sleep?

Anywhere he wants to.

How do you address a monster?

Very politely.

Why are monsters forgetful?
Because everything you tell them goes
in one ear and out the others.

^   x   x   x

What do ogres use to write with?
Ball point men.

^   x   x   x

What is large, yellow, lives in Scotland
and has never been seen?
The Loch Ness canary.

What happened when King Kong swallowed Big Ben?

He found it time-consuming.

Why did the monster knit herself three socks?
Because she grew another foot.

🌀 🌀 🌀

What's the difference between a huge, ugly, smelly
monster and a sweet?
People like sweets.

🌀 🌀 🌀

Which is the unluckiest monster in the world?
The Luck Less Monster.

🌀 🌀 🌀

What's a monster's favorite way to travel?
By bood vessel.

🌀 🌀 🌀

How can you mend King Kong's arm if he's twisted it?
With a monkey wrench.

🌀 🌀 🌀

What is Dr Jekyll's favorite game?
Hyde and Seek.

🌀 🌀 🌀

Did you know that Dr Jekyll has created
a new medicine?
One sip and you're a new man.

How did the monster cure his sore throat?
He spent all day gargoyling.

Where did Dr Jekyll find his best friend?
In Hyde Park.

Why did Frankenstein squeeze his girlfriend
to death?
He had a crush on her.

What did Dr Frankenstein get when he put his
goldfish's brain in the body of his dog?
I don't know, but it is great at chasing
submarines.

What did the Pharaohs use to keep their
babies quiet?
Egyptian dummies.

How did Dr frankenstein pay the men who built
his monster?
on a piece rate.

How do you raise a baby monster that has
been abandoned by its parents?
With a fork-lift truck.

How do you keep an ugly monster in suspense?
I'll tell you tomorrow....

What do you get if you cross a plum with a
man-eating monster?
A purple people-eater.

What will a monster eat in a restaurant?
The waiter.

How do man-eating monsters count to a
thousand?
On their warts.

~~~~~~~~~~

What's a man-eating monster's favorite
book?
Ghouliver's Travels.

~~~~~~~~~~

What do you call a one-eyed monster who
rides a motorbike?
Cycle-ops.

~~~~~~~~~~

Why did the big, hairy monster give up
boxing?
Because he didn't want to spoil his looks.

~~~~~~~~~~

What do you get if you cross a man-eating
monster with a skunk?
A very ugly smell.

What steps should you take if you see a
dangerous yeti on your travels?
Very large ones.

What do you get if you cross the Loch Ness
Monster with a shark?
Loch Jaws.

Where do you find wild yetis?
It depends where you left them.

How did the midget monster get into the
police force?
He lied about his height.

What do young female monsters do at
parties?
They go around looking for edible bachelors.

What happened to frankenstein's monster on the road?
He was stopped for speeding, fined $70 and dismantled for six months.

How did frankenstein's monster eat his lunch?
He bolted it down.

What's big, red and prickly, has three eyes and eats rocks?
A big, red, prickly, three-eyed, rock-eating monster.

What does frankenstein's monster call a screwdriver?
Daddy.

What do you call a clever monster?
Frank Einstein.

Why was Baron Frankenstein never lonely?
Because he was good at making fiends.

What do you get if you cross an Egyptian mummy with
a car mechanic?
Toot and car Man.

What eats its victims two by two?
Noah's Shark.

Why was the horrible big monster making a terrible
noise all night?
After eating Madonna he thought he could sing.

What do you get if you cross an elephant with the
abominable snowman?
A jumbo yeti.

Why did the cyclops give up teaching?
Because he only had one pupil.

Where is the monster's temple?
on the side of his head.

Why did the monster lie on his back?
To trip up low-flying aircraft.

What do you get if you cross a tall, green monster
with a fountain pen?
The Ink-credible Hulk.

How do you communicate with the Loch Ness
Monster at 20,000 fathoms?
Drop him a line.

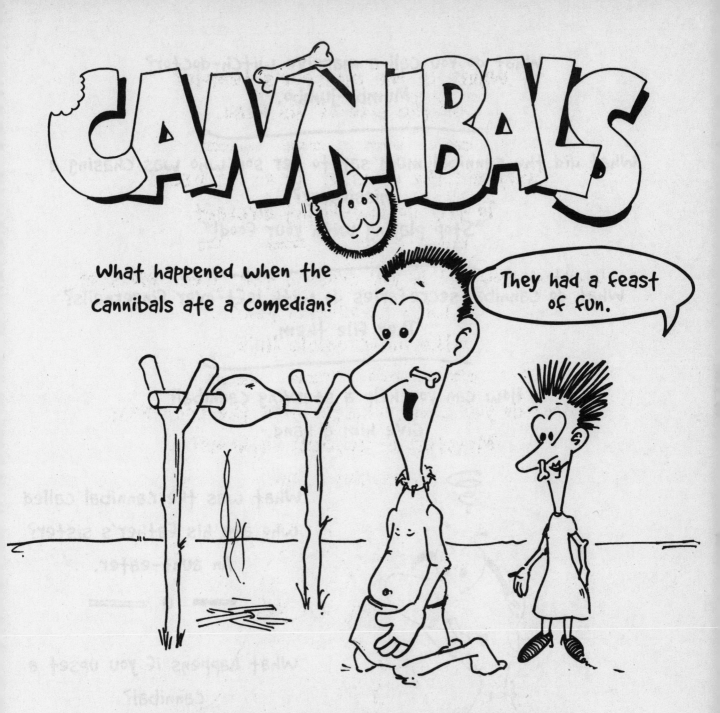

CANNIBALS

What happened when the cannibals ate a comedian?

They had a feast of fun.

What happened at the cannibal's wedding party?
They toasted the bride and groom.

When do cannibals cook you?
On fried-days.

What does a cannibal eat with cheese?
Pickled organs.

What do you call a massive witch-doctor?
Mumbo-jumbo.

What did the cannibal mum say to her son who was chasing a missionary?
"Stop playing with your food!"

What do cannibal secretaries do with left-over fingernails?
They file them.

How can you help a starving cannibal?
Give him a hand.

What was the cannibal called who ate his father's sister?
An aunt-eater.

What happens if you upset a cannibal?

You get into hot water.

What does a cannibal call a
skateboarder?
Meals on wheels.

What did the cannibal say when he
came home and found his wife
chopping up a python and a pygmy?
"Oh no, not snake and pygmy pie
again!"

What's the definition of a cannibal?
Someone who goes into a restaurant
and orders the waiter.

What do cannibals say when they say grace?
"We thank you, Lord, for our daily dead."

What did the cannibal say when he was full?
"I couldn't eat another mortal."

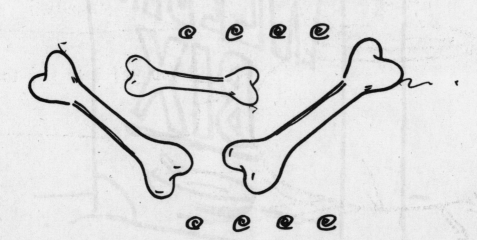

What did the cannibal say to the explorer?

"Nice to meat you!"

What did the cannibal make of her new friend?

A hotpot.

Why did the cannibal have a hangover?

He went to a party and got stewed.

Why was the cannibal fined $50 by the judge?

He was caught poaching.

What do pygmy cannibals eat for breakfast?

Weedie Bix.

What do cannibals eat at parties?
Buttered host.

How does a witch-doctor ask a girl to dance?
"Voodoo like to dance with me?"

What happened when the cannibal crossed the Atlantic on the QE2?
He told the waiter to take the menu away and bring him the passenger list.

Why don't cannibals like to eat Carl Lewis?
He gives them the runs.

What happened when the cannibal ate the speaking clock?
It repeated on him.

Why won't cannibals eat Frank Sinatra?
Because he's always coming back.

What do sick cannibals have for breakfast?
Vitamin Bills.

Why don't cannibals eat weathermen?
Because they give them wind.

What is a cannibal's favorite food?
Baked beings.

What happened when the cannibal got religion?
He only ate catholics on fridays.

Why would the cannibal only eat babies?
He was on a diet.

Why didn't the cannibal eat Mike Tyson?
He thought he would give him a paunch.

What happened when the cannibal bit off a missionary's ear?
He had his first taste of Christianity.

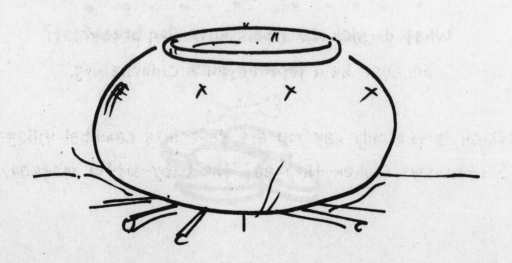

Why did the Scottish cannibal live on a sugar plantation? He said "So that I can feed my lads with m'lasses."

What did a cannibal's parents say when she brought her boyfriend home? "Lovely, dear, he looks good enough to eat!"

How did the cannibal turn over a new leaf?
He became a vegetarian.

Why was the cannibal looking peeky?
Because he'd just eaten a Chinese dog.

Which is the only day you are safe in a cannibal village?
Sitter days (when they eat the baby-sitter instead).

What happened to the
cannibal lion?
He had to swallow his pride.

Why did the cannibal live on
his own?
He was fed up with other
people.

Why do cannibals make
suitcases out of people's
heads?
Because they're headcases.

What is the cannibals' favorite game?
Swallow my leader.

What happened when a cannibal went on a self-catering holiday?
He ate himself.

What happened to the entertainer who did a show for an audience of
cannibals?
He went down really well.

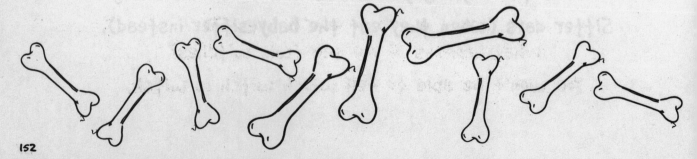

WITCHES

What is a witch with poison ivy called?
An itchy witchy.

What's a cold, evil candle called?
The wicked wick of the north.

What is evil, ugly and black and goes round and round?
A witch in a revolving door.

What is evil and ugly on the inside and green on the outside?
A witch dressed as a cucumber.

What happens if you see twin witches?
You won't be able to tell which witch is witch.

Why did the witch give up fortune telling?
There was no future in it.

○ ▭ ○ ▬ ○ ▬ ○ ▬ ○

Why did the baby witch smile when she came out in blotches?
Because it was an 'appy rash.

○ ▭ ○ ▬ ○ ▬ ○

What does a witch get if she's a poor traveler?
Broom sick.

○ ▭ ○ ▬ ○ ▬ ○ ▬ ○

How did the witch almost lose her baby?
She didn't take it far enough into the woods.

Why did the stupid
witch keep her clothes
in the fridge?

She liked to have
something cool to slip
into in the evening.

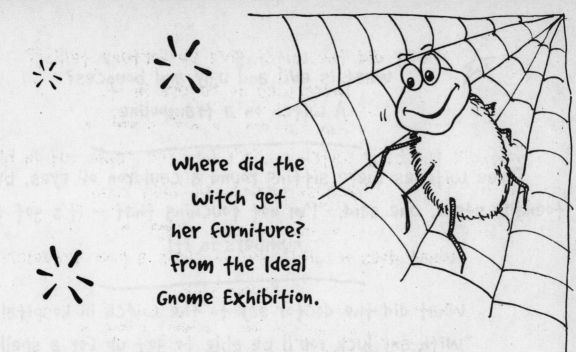

Where did the
witch get
her furniture?
from the Ideal
Gnome Exhibition.

Why did the witch put her broom in the washing
machine?
She wanted a clean sweep.

How did the witch feel when she got run
over by a car?
Tired.

What has six legs and flies?
A witch giving her cat a lift.

What has handles and flies?
A witch in a dustbin.

What is evil and ugly and bounces?
A witch on a trampoline.

Three witches were sitting round a cauldron of eyes, brain and toenails stew. One said, "I'm not touching that – it's got too many E-numbers in it!"

What did the doctor say to the witch in hospital?
"With any luck you'll be able to get up for a spell."

What do witches race on?
Vroomsticks.

What name did the witch give to her Cooking pot? It was Called—Ron.

How do witches lose weight?
They join weight witches.

Why do witches scratch themselves all the time?
Because they're the only ones who know where a witch itches.

Why did the witch wear a green felt pointed hat?
So she could walk across snooker tables without being seen.

How can you tell if a witch is really ugly?
When a wasp stings her he closes his eyes.

Why did the witch go over the mountain?
She couldn't go under it.

How do witches tell the time?
By looking at their witch watches.

What's the best way of talking to a warty witch?
On a long-distance telephone line.

How can you tell an Italian witch from an English one?
By her suntan.

What is evil and ugly and goes at 125mph?
A witch in a high-speed train.

How is the witches' team doing?
They're having a spell in the first division.

Have you heard about the good-weather witch?
She's forecasting sunny spells.

Why aren't we getting any sun then?
Because she can't spell "sunny."

What did one witch say to the other when they came out of the cinema?
"Do you want to walk home or shall we take the broom?"

What's a witch's favorite book?
Broom at the Top.

What's the witches' favorite pop group?
Broomski Beat.

What makes more noise than an angry witch?
Two angry witches.

What is the safest way to see a witch?
On television.

What did the witch write in her Christmas card?
Best vicious of the season.

What do you get if you cross a witch with a flea?
Very worried dogs.

What do little witches like to play at school?
Bat's cradle.

What happened to the witch with an upside down nose?
Every time she sneezed her hat blew off.

What happened when the baby witch was born?
It was so ugly its parents ran away from home.

What happened when the witch went for a job as a TV presenter?
The producer said she had the perfect face for radio.

What kind of music do witches play on the piano?
Hag-time.

What is old and ugly and can see just as well from both ends?
A witch with a blindfold.

Why did the witch
join Tottenham
Hotspur football club?
Because she heard
they needed a new
sweeper.

What do witches eat for breakfast?
Rice Krispies. Because they snap at them.

What do witches eat for dinner?
Real toad in the hole.

What is the best way of stopping infection from witch bites?
Don't bite any witches.

What should you expect if you drop in on a
witch's home unexpectedly?
Pot luck.

What do witches sing at Christmas?
"Deck the halls with poison ivy..."

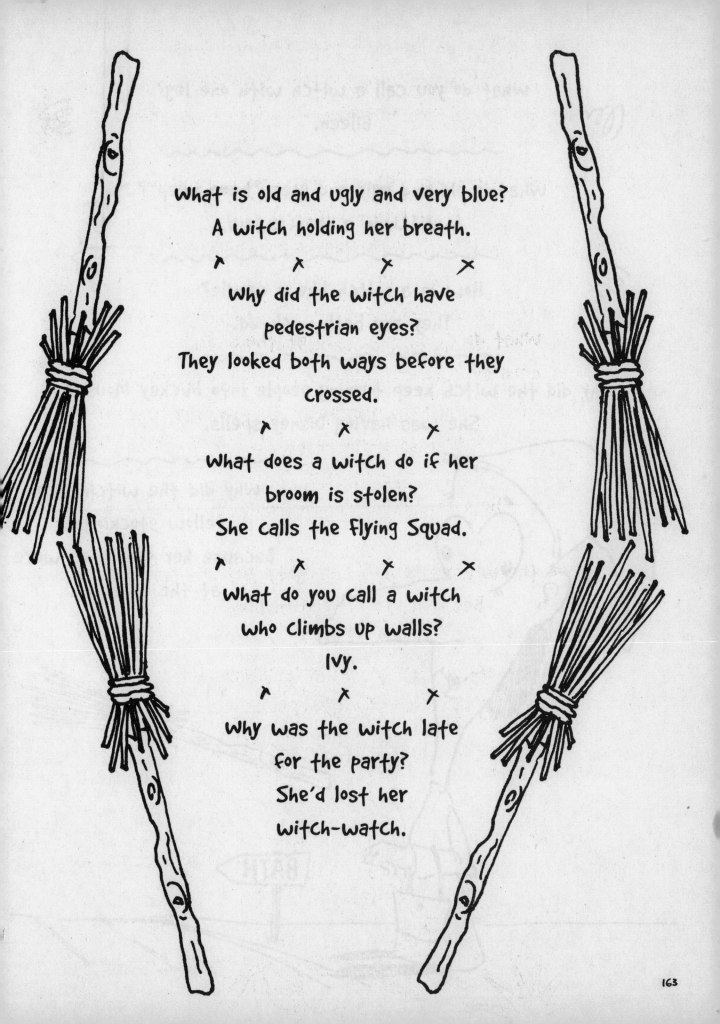

What is old and ugly and very blue?
A witch holding her breath.

∧   X   X   X

Why did the witch have
pedestrian eyes?
They looked both ways before they
crossed.

∧   X   X

What does a witch do if her
broom is stolen?
She calls the Flying Squad.

∧   X   X   X

What do you call a witch
who climbs up walls?
Ivy.

∧   X   X

Why was the witch late
for the party?
She'd lost her
witch-watch.

What do you call a witch with one leg?
Eileen.

What is old and ugly and goes "beep beep"?
A witch in a traffic jam.

How is a witch like a candle?
They are both wick-ed.

Why did the witch keep turning people into Mickey Mouse?
She was having Disney spells.

Why did the witch wear
yellow stockings?
Because her gray ones were
at the cleaners.

BATH

What goes cackle, cackle, squelch, squelch?
A witch in soggy trainers.

What usually runs in witches' families?
Noses.

What goes cackle, cackle, boom?
A witch in a minefield.

What happens to witches when it rains?
They get wet.

What is black and ugly and has four wheels?
A witch on a skateboard.

What do you call an old hag who lives by the sea?
A sand-witch.

~~~~~~~

What is the difference between a musician and a dead witch?
One composes and the other decomposes.

~~~~~~~

What do you get if you cross an owl with a witch?
A bird that's ugly but doesn't give a hoot.

~~~~~~~

Why did the witch go to the psychiatrist?
Because she thought everybody loved her.

~~~~~~~

Why won't a witch wear a flat cap?
Because there's no point in it.

What kind of flower is a witch's favorite?
A triffid.

Which of the witches' friends eats the fastest?
The goblin.

What do you call a witch that stays out all night?
A fresh air freak.

What do you get if you cross a witch with an iceberg?
A cold spell.

Why is the air so clean and healthy on Hallowe'en?
Because so many witches are sweeping the sky.

What do you call a witch by the side of the road with her thumb out?
A witch-hiker.

· · · · · · · ·

What's the favorite subject of young witches at school?
Spelling.

～～～～～～～～～～

Why did the witch consult an astrologer?
She wanted to know her horror-scope.

· · · · · · · ·

What's the difference between a witch and
the letters M A K E S?
one makes spells and the other spells "makes."

～～～～～～～～～～

What do little witches do after school?
Their gnomework.

· · · · · · · ·

Why do witches ride on broomsticks?
It's easier than walking.

What is the witches' favorite musical?
My Fear Lady.

~~~~~~~~~~

What is a witch's favorite drink?
Tea-hee-hee.

• • • • • •

What do witches say when they overtake each other?
"Broom, broom, broom."

~~~~~~~~~~

Why do witches get good bargains?
Because they like to haggle.

What's the difference between a deer running away and a small witch?
One's a hunted stag and the other's a stunted hag.

Why did the young witch have such difficulty writing letters?
She had never learnt to spell properly.

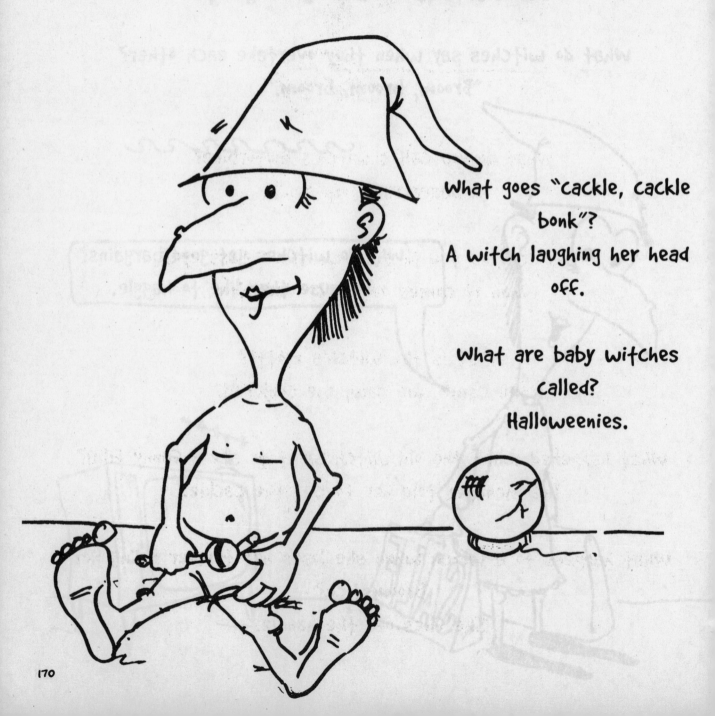

What goes "cackle, cackle bonk"?
A witch laughing her head off.

What are baby witches called?
Halloweenies.

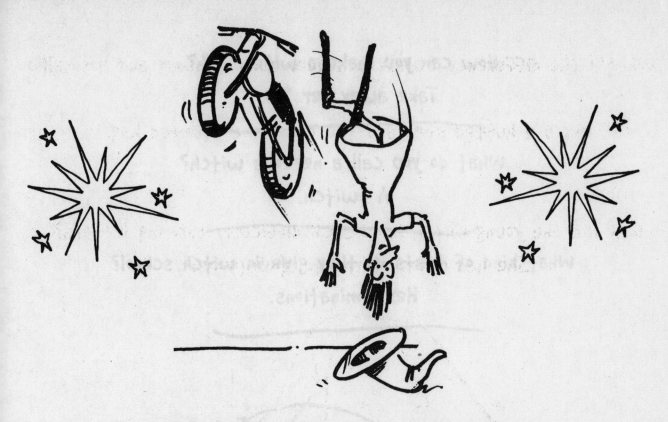

What do you call a witch's motorbike?
A baaaarrrooooom stick.

How can you tell if a witch has a glass eye?
When it comes out in conversation.

What is the witch's motto?
We came, we saw, we conjured.

What happened when the old witch went to see a funny film?
The manager told her to cut the cackle.

What happens to a witch when she loses her temper riding her
broomstick?
She flies off the handle.

How can you make a witch itch?
Take away her "w."

What do you call a nervous witch?
A twitch.

What kind of tests do they give in witch school?
Hex-aminations.

What do you get if you cross a sorceress with a millionaire?
A very witch person.

How do witches on broomsticks drink their tea?
Out of flying saucers.

Where does a witch keep her purse?
In a hag bag.

What do witches ring for in a hotel?
B-room service.

Who's the fastest witch?
The one that rides on a vroooooom stick.

Why do witches fly on broomsticks?
Because vacuum cleaners are too heavy.

What kind of jewelry do warty witches wear on their wrists?
Charm bracelets.

^   x   x   x

How do you know when you're in bed with a witch?
She has a big "W" embroidered on her pyjamas.

^   x   x   x

When should you feed witch's milk to a baby?
When it's a baby witch.

^   x   x   x

If a flying saucer is an aircraft, does that make a flying broom a witchcraft?

^   x   x   x

Why didn't the witch sing at the concert?
Because she had a frog in her throat.

What do you call a witch who drives really badly?
A road hag.

~~~~~~~~~~~~

What do you call a witch who is made of cotton and has lots of holes in her?
A string hag.

~~~~~~~~~~~~

What should you do if you find a witch in your bed?
Run!

~~~~~~~~~~~~

What happened to the naughty little witch at school?
She was ex-spelled.

~~~~~~~~~~~~

Why did the witch buy two tickets to the zoo?
One to get in and one to get out.

What noise do witches make when they cry?
They go, "Brew-hoo! Brew-hoo!"

o   o   o   o

Why should men be careful of beautiful witches?
They'll sweep them off their feet.

^   x   x   x

Is it true that a witch won't hurt you if you run away
from her?
It all depends on how fast you run!

o   o   o   o

What do you call a witch who kills her mother and father?
An orphan.

^   x   x   x

How does a witch make scrambled eggs?
She holds the pan and gets two friends to make the stove
shake with fright.

Where is the witch's temple?
on each side of her head.

❤ ❤ ❤ ❤ ❤ ❤

Why do some witches eat raw meat?
Because they don't know how to cook.

◇ ◇ ◇

How do you make a witch float?
Take two scoops of ice cream, a
glass of coke and one witch...

❤ ❤ ❤ ❤ ❤ ❤

What's yellow and very
poisonous?
Witch-infested custard.

◇ ◇ ◇

What does a witch enjoy
cooking most?
Gnomelettes.

What do baby witches play with?
Deady bears.

~~~~~~~~~~~~~~~~

How can you tell when witches are carrying a time bomb?
You can hear their brooms tick!

How do warty witches keep their hair out of place?
With scare spray.

~~~~~~~~~~~~~~~~

Why is "S" the witches' favorite letter?
Because it turns cream into scream.

What do you call a pretty and friendly witch?
A failure.

Why are witches' fingernails never more than 11 inches long?
Because if they were 12 inches they'd be a foot.

What do you call a witch who flies in Concorde?
Lucky.

What is evil and ugly, puts spells on people and is made of leaves?
A witch (the leaves were just a plant).

What does a witch turn into when the lights go out?
The dark.

Why do witches go to the docks?
To see the bats being launched.

What do you do if a witch in a pointy hat sits in front of you in the cinema?
Miss most of the film.

How is a witch's face like a million dollars?
It's all green and wrinkly.

What's evil and ugly and goes up and down all day?
A witch in a lift.

What do you call a which who likes the beach but is scared of the water?
A chicken sand-witch.

Why did the witches go on strike?
Because they wanted sweeping reforms.

Who went into a witch's den and came out alive?
The witch.

What do you call two witches who share a broomstick?
Broom-mates.

What do witches use pencil sharpeners for?
To keep their hats pointed.

What is evil, ugly and keeps the
neighbors awake?
A witch with a drumkit.

Why do witches have stiff joints?
They get broomatism.

Why did the witch ride on a french duster?
She felt like a dust-up.

When a witch falls into a pond what is the first
thing that she does?
Gets wet.

What would you say if you saw nine witches in black capes
flying south and one witch in a red cape flying north?
That nine out of ten witches wear black capes.

Why couldn't the young witch write a decent letter?
Because she couldn't spell properly.

Why do witches only ride their broomsticks after dark?
That's the time to go to sweep.

What turns off the lights on Halloween?
The light's witch.

What did the witch say to the ugly toad?
"I'd put a curse on you - but somebody beat me to it!"

What's the difference between a broomstick and a pumpkin?
You can't make broomstick pie.

What's the best advice you can give to a witch on a broomstick?
"Don't fly off the handle!"

What is a witch's favorite magazine?
The Witch Report.

What did the young
witch say to her
mother?
"Can I have the keys
to the broom
tonight?"

Why does a witch
wear a pointed black
hat?
To keep her head
warm.

WITCHES' CATS

Why are black cats such good singers?
They're very mewsical.

When is it unlucky to see a black cat?
When you're a mouse.

What do you get if you cross a witch's cat with father christmas?
Santa claws.

How do you get milk from a witch's cat?
Steal her saucer.

What do witch's cats like for breakfast?
Mice Krispies.

— o — o · ·

What do you get if you cross a witch's cat with a canary?
A peeping tom.

— — — —

Why did the witch feed her cat with pennies?
She wanted to put some money in the kitty.

— o — o — o

What is an octopus?
An eight-sided cat.

Why do black cats never
shave?
Because eight out of ten
cats prefer Whiskas.

— o — o ·

What do you call it when a
witch's cat falls off her
broomstick?
A catastrophe.

What did the black cat say to the fish?
I've got a bone to pick with you.

Why is a witch's kitten like an unhealed wound?
Both are a little pussy.

What do you call a witch's cat that drinks vinegar?
A sour puss.

What do you call a witch's cat who never comes when she's called?
Im-puss-able.

"Now you see it...now you don't" - what are you looking at?
A black cat walking over a zebra crossing.

What do you call a witch's cat with no legs?
Anything you like - she won't be able to chase you.

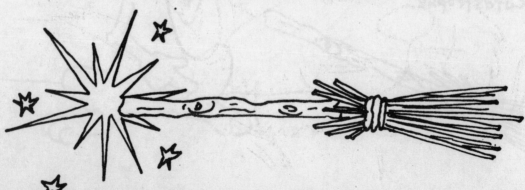

What's furry, has whiskers and chases outlaws?
A posse cat.

What do you get if you cross a witch's cat and a canary?
A cat with a full tummy.

What is a black cat's favorite TV show?
Miami Mice.

What has four legs, a tail, whiskers and cuts grass?
A lawn miaower.

What has four legs, a tail, whiskers and goes
round and round for hours?
A black cat in a tumble-drier.

What do you call a witch's cat who can spring from the
ground to her mistress's hat in one leap?
A good jum-purr.

What do you call a witch's cat who can do spells as well as her mistress?
An ex-purr-t.

What did one black cat say to the other?
Nothing. Cats can't speak.

What did the black cat do when its tail was cut off?
It went to a re-tail store.

Why did the witch lose her way?
Because her hat was pointing in the wrong direction.

What do witches' cats strive for?
Purr-fection.

Ding dong bell,
Pussy's down the well,
We've put some disinfectant
down
And don't mind the smell.

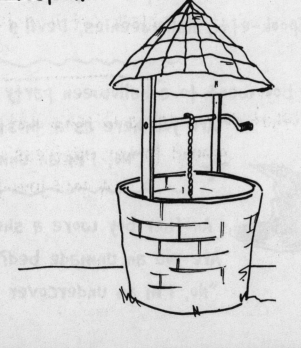

HALLOWEEN

Why are teachers happy at Halloween parties?
Because there's lots of school spirit.

What happened to the girl who wore a mouse costume to her
Halloween party?
The cat ate her.

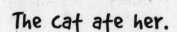

What do witches eat at Halloween?
Spook-etti, Halloweenies, Devil's food cake and Boo-berry pie.

A boy went to a Halloween party with a sheet over his head.
"Are you here as a ghost?" said his friends.
"No, I'm an unmade bed."

Another boy wore a sheet over his head.
"Are you an unmade bed?" asked his friends.
"No, I'm an undercover agent," he replied.

What did the really ugly man do for a living?
He posed for Halloween masks.

Why did the ghost go trick or treating on
the top floor?
He was in high spirits.

Why did the girl dressed
as a spoon left
the Halloween party?
No one moved. They couldn't stir without her.

Why was the boy unhappy to win the prize for
the best costume at the Halloween party?
Because he just came to pick up his little sister.

Why was everyone tickled by the fried chicken at
a Halloween party?
Because the feathers were still on the chicken.

Why did the boy carry a clock and a bird on Halloween?
It was for "tick or tweet."

What do stupid kids do at Halloween?
They carve a face on an apple and go bobbing for pumpkins.

Why don't apples smile when you go bobbing?
Because they're crab apples.

How do you get the most apples at Halloween?
Take a snorkel.

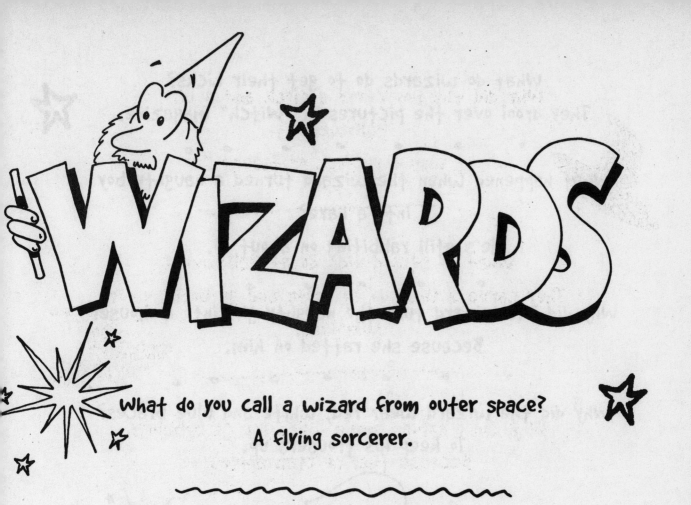

WIZARDS

What do you call a wizard from outer space?
A flying sorcerer.

~~~~~~~~~~~~~~~~~~~~~~~~

Why did the wizard wear a yellow robe to the
Halloween party?
He was going as a banana.

~~~~~~~~~~~~~~~~~~~~~~~~

What happened to the stupid wizard who put his false
teeth in the wrong way round?
He ate himself.

~~~~~~~~~~~~~~~~~~~~~~~~

What happened to the wizard who brushed his teeth with
gunpowder?
He kept shooting his mouth off.

What do wizards do to get their kicks?
They drool over the pictures in "Witch" magazine.

• • • • • •

What happened when the wizard turned a naughty boy
into a hare?
He's still rabbiting on about it.

• • • • •

Why did the wizard turn the naughty girl into a mouse?
Because she ratted on him.

• • • • • •

Why did the wizard wear red, white and blue braces?
To keep his trousers up.

What is the first thing a wizard does in the morning?
He wakes up.

What did the wizard say to his witch girlfriend?
Hello gore-juice!

What do wizards stop for on the motorway?
Witch-hikers.

Why do cats prefer wizards to witches?
Because the sorcerers often have milk in them.

Why did the wizard jump off the top of the Empire State building?
He wanted to make a hit on Broadway.

What do you get if you cross a river with an inflatable wizard?
To the other side.

What do you get if you cross a dinosaur with a wizard?
Tyrannosaurus hex.

What do you call a wizard who's black and blue all over?
Bruce.

What do you call a wizard who lies on the floor?
Matt.

What do you call a wizard lying in the gutter?
Dwayne.

Who did the wizard marry?
His ghoul-friend.

How do you keep a wizard in suspense?
I'll tell you tomorrow...

What kinds of wizards have their eyes closest together?
The smallest ones.

Why does a wizard clean his teeth three times a day?
To prevent bat breath.

↑ ✗ ✗

What happened to the wizard who ran away with the circus?
The police made him bring it back again.

↑ ✗ ✗ ✗

What do you call a wizard who has fallen into the sea in a barrel?
Bob.

↑ ✗ ✗

What do you call a warlock who tries to stop fights?
A Peacelock.

What must a wizard be to receive a state funeral?

Dead.

What kinds of wizards can jump higher than a bus?

All kinds - busses can't jump.

What happened when the young wizard met the young witch?

It was love at first fright.

If a wizard were knocked out by Dracula in a fight what would he be?

Out for the count.

What would happen if you threw lots of eggs at a wizard?

He would be egg-sterminated.

What did the wizard say at the end of a long, hard day?

I'm going gnome.

What happened when the wizard drank ten bottles of lemonade?

He burped 7-Up.

VAMPIRES

What do you call a dog owned by Dracula?
A blood hound.

Why does Dracula have no friends?
Because he's a pain in the neck.

What was the
californian hippie
vampire like?
He was ghoul man.
Real ghoul.

What's a vampire's
favorite sport?
Batminton.

What happened to the two mad vampires?
They both went a little batty.

What do vampires have at eleven o'clock every day?
A coffin break.

What do vampire footballers have at half-time?
Blood oranges.

How does Dracula like to have his food served?
In bite-sized pieces.

Where do vampires go on holiday?
The Isle of fright.

Why did the vampire take up acting?
It was in his blood.

ISLE OF FRIGHT

Who plays center forward for the vampire football team?
The ghoulscorer.

What's a vampire's favorite soup?
Sharks' fang soup.

What happened to the lovesick vampire?
He became a neck-romancer.

What do you get if you cross a vampire with a snail?
I don't know but it would slow him down.

◇   ◇   ◇

Which vampire ate the three bears' porridge?
Gouldilocks.

◇   ◇

Why did the vampire go to hospital?
He wanted his ghoulstones removed.

◇   ◇   ◇

Why did the vampire stand at the bus stop with his finger up his nose
He was a ghoulsniffer.

◇   ◇

What's a vampire's favorite drink?
A Bloody Mary.

◇   ◇   ◇

What is the vampire's favorite dance?
The Fangdango.

◇   ◇

Which vampire tried to eat James Bond?
Ghouldfinger.

What does a vampire say when you tell him a ghoul joke?
Ghoul blimey!

◇   ◇   ◇

When do vampires bite you?
On Wincedays.

◇   ◇

What do vampires think of blood transfusions?
New-fang-led rubbish.

Why did the vampire baby
stop having baby food?
He wanted something to
get his teeth into.

Why did the vampire enjoy ballroom dancing?
He could really get into the vaultz.

_____

What happened at the vampires' race?
They finished neck and neck.

_____

Where did vampires go to first in America?
New-fang-land.

What happened at the vampires' reunion?
All the blood relations went.

What do you get if you cross Dracula with Al Capone?
A fangster.

_____

Where do Chinese vampires come from?
Fanghai.

What do vampires sing on New Year's Eve?
"Auld Fang Syne."

What is Dracula's favorite fruit?
Neck-tarines.

Why did Dracula go to the dentist?
He had fang decay.

What did Dracula
say to the
Wolfman?
"You look like
you're going to
the dogs."

What is the American national day for vampires?

Why did he have fang decay?
He was always eating fangcy cakes.

If you want to know more about Dracula what do you have to do?
Join his fang club.

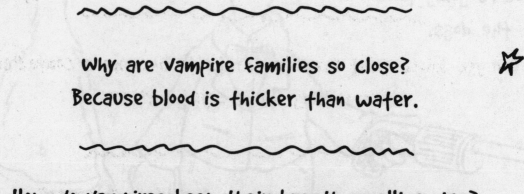

Why are vampire families so close?
Because blood is thicker than water.

How do vampires keep their breath smelling nice?
They use extractor fangs.

Fangsgiving Day.

What does Dracula say when you tell him a new fact?
"Well, fangcy that!"

Why was Dracula thought of as being polite?
He always said "fangs."

Did you know that Dracula wants to become a comedian?
He's looking for a crypt writer.

Which flavor ice-cream is Dracula's favorite?
Vein-illa.

Why did the vampire attack the clown?
He wanted the circus to be in his blood.

What is the first thing that vampires learn at school?
The alphabat.

Why did Dracula go to the orthodontist?
He wanted to improve his bite.

Why is Hollywood full of vampires?
They need someone to play the bit parts.

Why wouldn't the vampire eat his soup?
It clotted.

Why are vampires always exhausted in April?
Because they've just completed a long March of 31 days.

— o — o — .

Why did the vampire sit on a pumpkin?
It wanted to play squash.

— o — o — .

Why do vampires like school dinners?
Because they know they won't get stake.

What do you get if you cross a Rolls Royce with a vampire?
A monster that attacks expensive cars and sucks out their gas tanks.

How do you join the Dracula fan club?
Send your name, address and blood group.

What's a vampire's favorite animal?
A giraffe.

DE-
COFFINATED

Why was the young vampire a failure?
Because he fainted at the sight of blood.

Why did the vampire give up acting?
He couldn't get his teeth into the part.

What happened to the vampire who swallowed a sheep?
He felt baaaaaaaaaaaaaad.

What does Mrs Dracula say to Mr Dracula when he leaves for
work in the evening?
"Have a nice bite!"

What's Dracula's favorite coffee?
De-coffin-ated.

What do you get if you cross Dracula with Sir Lancelot?
A bite in shining armor.

What's Dracula's car called?
A mobile blood unit.

Why do vampires do well at school?
Because every time they're asked a question they come up with a biting reply.

What does a vampire bath in?
A bat tub.

Why are vampires crazy?
Because they're often bats.

What did the vampire say when he had been to the dentist?
"Fangs very much."

What kind of medicine does Dracula take for a cold?
Coffin medicine.

How does a vampire clean his house?
With a victim cleaner.

Where is Dracula's American office?
The Vampire State Building.

What does the postman deliver to vampires?
Fang mail.

What do you get if you cross a vampire with a jar of peanut butter?
A vampire that sticks to the roof of your mouth.

What is a vampire's favorite soup?
Scream of tomato.

What's the difference between a vampire and a biscuit?
Have you ever tried dunking a vampire in your tea?

What did the vampire sing to the doctor who cured him of amnesia?
"Fangs for the Memory."

~~~~~~~~~~~~~~~~

What does a vampire stand on after taking a shower?
A bat mat.

What's a vampire's
favorite dance?
The Vaults.

~~~~~~~~~~~~~~~~

What do romantic
vampires do?
Neck.

~~~~~~~~~~~~~~~~

What do you call a
vampire junkie?
Count Drugula.

~~~~~~~~~~~~~~~~

Where do vampires keep
their savings?
In blood banks.

What did the vampire call his false teeth?
A new fangled device.

What did Dracula say to his new apprentice?
"We could do with some new blood around here."

Why do vampires hate arguments?
Because they make themselves cross.

What happened when the vampire went to the bloodbank?
He asked to make a withdrawal.

What's a vampire's favorite love song?
"How Can I Ignore the Girl Necks Door."

What did Dracula call his daughter?
Bloody Mary.

What does a vampire say to the mirror?
"Terror, terror on the wall."

~~~~~~~~~~~~~~~~~~~~~~~~~~~~~~~~~

What's a vampire's favorite cartoon character?
Batman.

~~~~~~~~~~~~~~~~~~~~~~~~~~~~~~~~~

Why do vampires eat in
transport cafes?
They can eat for necks to
nothing in them.

~~~~~~~~~~~~~~~~~~~~~~~~~~~~~~~~~

What type of people do vampires
like?
o positive people.

~~~~~~~~~~~~~~~~~~~~~~~~~~~~~~~~~

Why do people hate being bitten by
vampires?
Because it's a drain in the neck.

What do vampires play poker for?
High stakes.

Why do vampires drink blood?
Lemonade makes them burp.

Why do vampires like playing baseball?
Because they've got plenty of bats.

What kind of sausages do
vampires like best?
Fang-furters.

When the picture of the vampire's grandfather crashed to the floor in the middle of the night what did it mean?
That the nail had come out of the wall.

What do you get when a vampire bites a rat?
A neighborhood free of cats.

What kind of typewriters do vampires like?
Blood type-writers.

What is the best way to see a vampire?
On television.

What did the vampire say when he saw the neck of the sleeping man?
"Ah! Breakfast in bed."

What did the vampire do after he'd been to a party?
He sent a fang-you note.

How does a vampire get through life with only one fang?
He has to grin and bare it.

What do you call a vampire who gets up your nose?
Vic.

Which old song did Dracula hate?
"Peg o' My Heart."

What is Dracula's
favorite pudding?
Leeches and scream.

What sort of soup do vampires like?
One with plenty of body in it.

Why did Dracula miss lunch?
Because he didn't fancy the stake.

What is ugly, scary and very blue?
A vampire holding his breath.

Why did the vampire have pedestrian eyes?
They looked both ways before they crossed.

What do you call a vampire after it is one-year-old?
A two-year-old vampire.

What's it called when a vampire kisses you goodnight?
Necking.

Why does Dracula live in a coffin?
Because the rent is low.

Why was the vampire thought of as simple-minded?
Because he was a complete sucker.

How can you tell if a vampire's been at the tomato juice?
There are teeth marks on the lid.

What's the name of Dracula's cook?
Fangy Craddock.

What do vampires cross the sea in?
Blood vessels.

When he's out driving, where does Dracula like to stop and eat?
The Happy Biter.

Where do vampires go fishing?
In the blood stream.

What do you call a short vampire?
A pain in the knee.

What's a vampire's favorite hobby?
In-grave-ing.

What is red, sweet and bites people in the neck?
A jampire.

What do you get if you cross a vampire with a mummy?
A flying bandage.

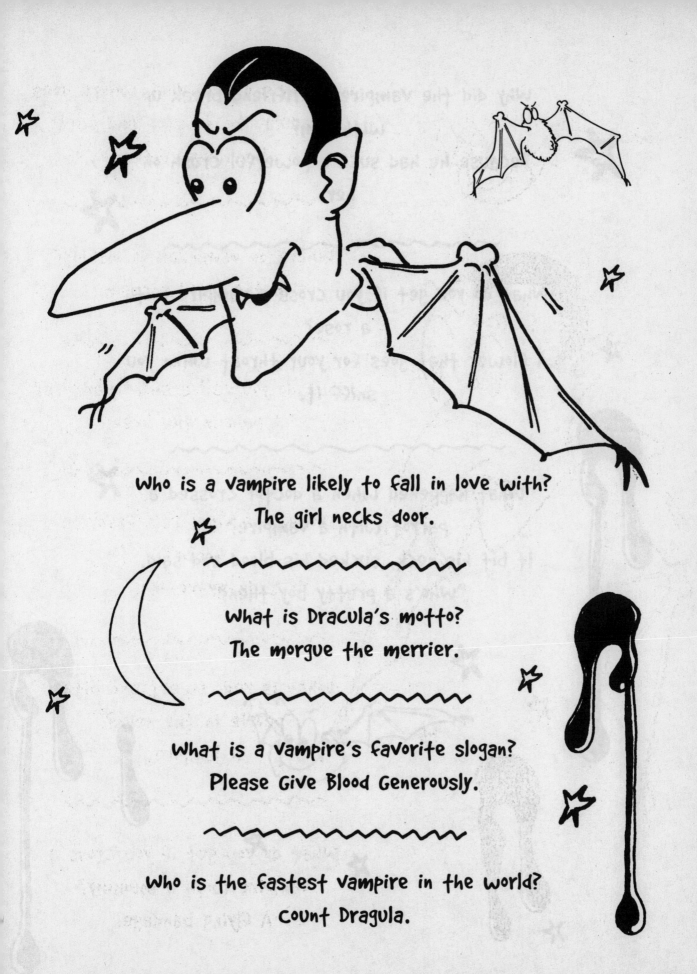

Who is a vampire likely to fall in love with?
The girl necks door.

What is Dracula's motto?
The morgue the merrier.

What is a vampire's favorite slogan?
Please Give Blood Generously.

Who is the fastest vampire in the world?
Count Dragula.

Why did the vampire's girlfriend break up with him?
Because he had such a powerful crush on her.

~~~~~~~~~~~~~~~~~~~~~~~~~~~~~~~~~~

What do you get if you cross a vampire with a rose?
A flower that goes for your throat when you sniff it.

~~~~~~~~~~~~~~~~~~~~~~~~~~~~~~~~~~

What happened when a doctor crossed a parrot with a vampire?
It bit his neck, sucked his blood and said, "Who's a pretty boy then?"

VULTURES

What do you do with sick vultures?
Have them tweeted.

Why did the vulture cross the road?
For a fowl reason.

Why don't vultures fly south in the winter?
Because they can't afford the air fare.

Why did a man's pet vulture not
make a sound for five years?
It was stuffed.

What do you call a team of vultures playing
football?
Fowl play.

Where do vultures meet for coffee?
In a nest-cafe.

⋏ ⋏ ⋏ ⋏

Where do the toughest vultures come from?
Hard-boiled eggs.

⋏ ⋏ ⋏ ⋏

What do you call a vulture with no beak?
A head-banger.

Why couldn't the vulture talk to the dove?
Because he didn't speak pigeon English.

⋏ ⋏ ⋏ ⋏

How do we know vultures are religious?
Because they're birds of prey.

⋏ ⋏ ⋏ ⋏

What do a vulture, a pelican and a taxman
have in common?
Big bills!

ZOMBIES

Why do zombies learn Latin?
Because they like dead languages.

Who do zombie cowboys fight?
Deadskins.

What did the zombie's friend say
when he introduced him to his
girlfriend?
"Where did you dig her up from?"

Why did the zombie go to
hospital?
He wanted to learn a few
sick jokes.

What do you call zombies in a belfry?
Dead ringers.

What do you find in a zombie's veins?
Dead blood corpuscles.

What does a zombie say when he gets a letter from his girlfriend?
It's a dead-letter day.

Where do zombies go for cruises?
The Deaditerranean.

What did the zombie get his medal for?
Deadication.

What happened to the zombie who had a bad cold?
He said, "I'm dead-up wid fuddy jokes aboud zondies."

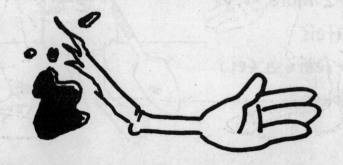

What do little zombies play?
Corpses and Robbers.

@ @

Why was the zombie's nightclub a disaster?
It was a dead and alive hole.

@ @

How do you know a zombie is tired?
He's dead on his feet.

@ @

What happened
when a vicar
saw a zombie
with nothing on
his neck?
He made a bolt
for it.

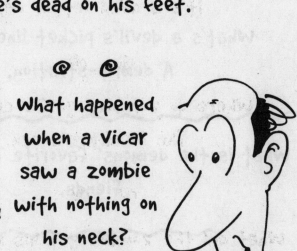

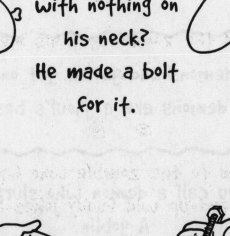

DEMONS

What's a devil's picket line called?
A demon-stration.

What is the demons' favorite TV sit-com?
Fiends.

Why do demons and ghouls get on so well?
Because demons are a ghoul's best friend.

What do you call a demon who slurps his food?
A goblin.

What is the best way to get rid of a demon?
Exorcise a lot.

What do foreign devils speak?
Devil dutch.

~~~~~~~~~~~~~~~~~~~~~~~~~~~~~~

A little demon came running into the house saying
"Mum, Dad's fallen on the bonfire!"
Mum said, "Great, we'll have a barbecue."

~~~~~~~~~~~~~~~~~~~~~~~~~~~~~~

What did the little demon do when he bought a house?
He called it Gnome Sweet Gnome.

~~~~~~~~~~~~~~~~~~~~~~~~~~~~~~

What do demons have for breakfast?
Deviled eggs.

~~~~~~~~~~~~~~~~~~~~~~~~~~~~~~

What do demons have on holiday?
A devil of a time.

GHOULIES

When can't you bury people who live opposite a graveyard?
When they're not dead.

What trees do ghouls like best?
ceme-trees.

What did the baby ghost eat for dinner?
A boo-loney sandwich.

Why are graveyards so noisy?
Because of all the coffin.

How can you tell if a corpse is angry?
It flips its lid.

Why are cemeteries in the middle of towns?
Because they're dead centers.

~~~~~~~~~~~~~~~~~~~~

Where do undertakers go in October?
The Hearse of the Year Show.

~~~~~~~~~~~~~~~~~~~~

How do undertakers speak?
Gravely.

~~~~~~~~~~~~~~~~~~~~

What do you get if you cross a
skeleton with a famous detective?
Sherlock bones.

~~~~~~~~~~~~

What was written on
the hypochondriac's
tombstone?
"I told you I was ill."

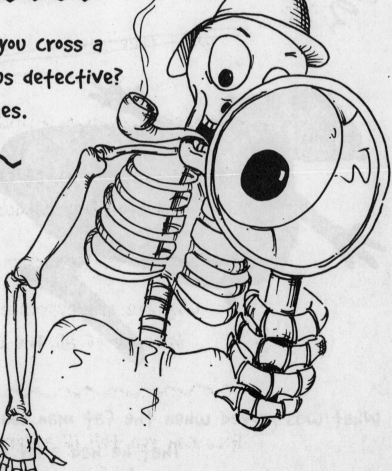

~~~~~~~~

What is a drunkard's last
drink?
His bier.

233

How did the glamorous ghoul earn her living?
She was a cover ghoul.

What do young ghosts write their homework in?
Exorcise books.

What keeps ghouls cheerful?
The knowledge that every shroud has a silver lining.

What was proved when the fat man was run over by a steamroller?
That he had a lot of guts.

What kind of girl does a mummy take on a date?
Any old girl he can dig up.

What do ghouls do when they're in hospital?
Talk about their apparitions.

What do you call a ghost's mother and father?
Transparents.

How did the ghost song-and-dance act make a living?
By appearing in television spooktaculars.

Where do mummies go if they want to swim?
The Dead Sea.

Why were ancient Egyptian children confused?
Because their daddies were mummies.

Why did the mummy leave his tomb
after 3000 years?
Because he thought he was old
enough to leave home.

What are little ghosts dressed in when it rains?
Boo-ts and ghoul-oshes.

Why are ghosts bad at telling lies?
Because you can see right through them.

Where does Sitting Bull's ghost live?
In a creepy teepee.

Who writes ghosts' jokes?
Crypt writers.

What kind of street does a ghost like best?
A dead end.

What do ghosts dance to?
Soul music.

What did the papa ghost say to the baby ghost?
Fasten your sheet belt.

Where do ghosts go on holiday?
The Ghosta Brava.

What did the ghost teacher say to her class?
"Watch the board and I'll go through it again."

What do you call a ghost that stays out all night?
A fresh air freak.

What happened when the ghosts went on strike?
A skeleton staff took over.

· · · · · · ·

What do ghosts say when a girl footballer is sent off?
Ban-she, ban-she!

· · · · ·

What is a ghost-proof bicycle?
One with no spooks in it.

· · · · · · ·

Why did the car judder to a stop when it saw a ghost?
It had a nervous breakdown.

· · · · ·

Where do ghost trains stop?
At devil crossings.

· · · · · ·

Why did the ghost go to the funfair?
He wanted to go on the rollerghoster.

· · · · ·

This woman wanted to marry a ghost.
I can't think what possessed her.

What do ghosts have in the front
seats of their cars?
Sheet belts.

How do ghosts learn songs?
They read the sheet music.

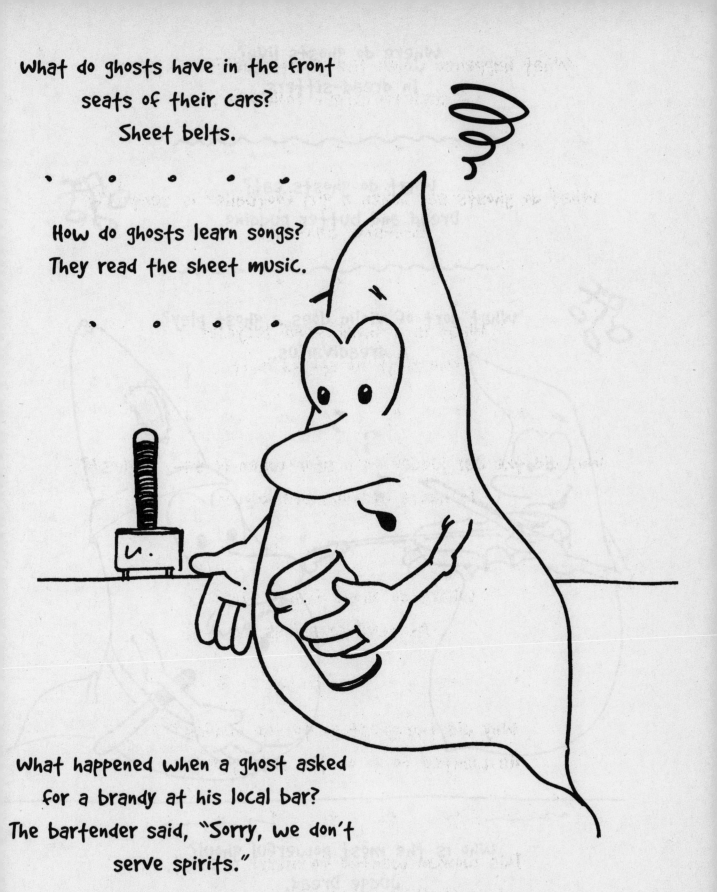

What happened when a ghost asked
for a brandy at his local bar?
The bartender said, "Sorry, we don't
serve spirits."

Where do ghosts live?
In dread-sitters.

What do ghosts eat?
Dread and butter pudding.

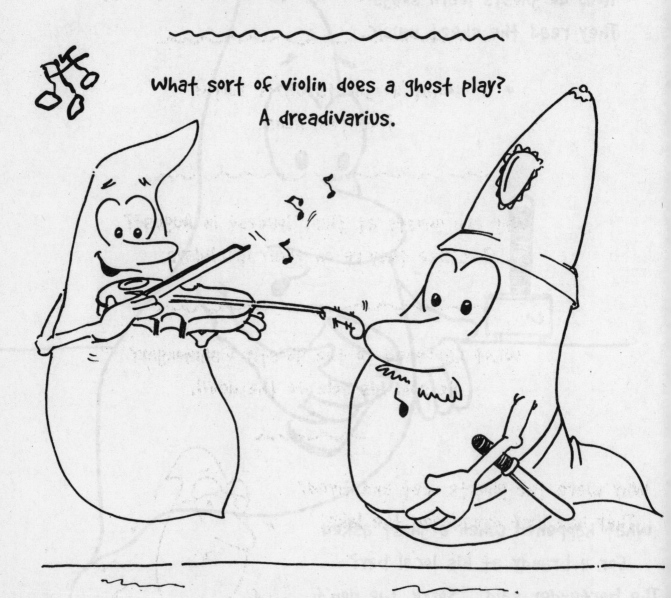

What sort of violin does a ghost play?
A dreadivarius.

Who is the most powerful ghoul?
Judge Dread.

Why did the ghost work at Scotland Yard?
He was the Chief In-Spectre.

~~~~~~~~~~~~~~~~

Why don't you get locks on cemetary gates?
There's no point - all the ghosts have skeleton keys.

~~~~~~~~~~~~~~~~

What do ghosts write with?
Phantom pens.

~~~~~~~~~~~~~~~~

Why are ghosts at their loudest in August?
Because they're on their howlidays.

~~~~~~~~~~~~~~~~

What happened to the ghostly fishmonger?
He sold his sole to the devil.

~~~~~~~~~~~~~~~~

Why were the ghosts wet and tired?
They had just dread-ged the lake.

What do you call the ghost who is a child-rearing expert?
Dr Spook.

Where do ghosts live?
In a terrortory.

What do you call a prehistoric ghost?
A terror-dactyl.

Classified advertisement:
For sale. 1926 hearse. Excellent condition; original body.

How can you tell you are talking to an undertaker?
By his grave manner.

How do you know you are haunted by a parrot?
He keeps saying "oooo's a pretty boy then?"

How do ghosts like their drinks?
Ice ghoul.

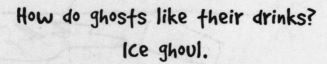

Where do ghosts get an education?
High s-ghoul.

What do ghosts eat for dinner?
Ghoulash.

Which airline do ghouls fly with?
United Scareways.

What kind of ghoul has the best hearing?
The eeriest.

What's a ghost's favorite day of the week?
Frightday.

How do ghouls keep fit?
By regular exorcise.

Who's the most important member in the ghosts' soccer team?
The Ghoulie.

How do ghouls like their eggs cooked?
Terrifried.

— — —

Where do Australian ghosts go on holiday?
Lake Eerie.

— — —

What did the polite ghost say to her son?
"Don't spook until you're spooken to."

— — —

What kind of ghosts haunt operating theaters?
Surgical spirits.

— — —

What kind of jewels do ghosts wear?
Tombstones.

— —

What's a ghost's favorite dessert?
Knickerbocker Ghouly.

— — —

What do you have to take to become a coroner?
A stiff exam.

When do ghosts play tricks on each other?
on April Ghoul's Day.

o ━━ o ━━

How do you make a ghoul float?
Two scoops of ice-cream, a bottle of coke and a slice of ghoul.

━━ o ━━ o o ━━

When do banshees howl?
on Moanday night.

o ━━ o ━━

What do ghosts see at the theater?
A phantomime.

━━ o ━━ o o ━━

What's a ghost's favorite type of art?
A ghoulage.

o ━━ o ━━

Who mans the ghoul's ship?
A skeleton crew.

━━ o ━━ o ━━ o

What do drunken ghosts drink?
Any kind of spirits.

What song does a ghost sing to warn people that he's around?
"Beware My Ghoulish Heart."

What's a ghost's favorite Beatles' song?
"The Ghoul on the Hill."

Which ghost was president of France?
Charles de Ghoul.

~~~~~~~~~~~~~~~~~~~~~

What should gymnasts do if they find themselves in a haunted house?
Exorcise.

~~~~~~~~~~~~~~~~~~~~~

What's the result of smoking too much?
Coffin.

~~~~~~~~~~~~~~~~~~~~~

What happened to the ghost who went to a party?
He had a wail of a time.

~~~~~~~~~~~~~~~~~

What ghost is handy in the kitchen?
A recipe spook.

~~~~~~~~~~~~~~~~~

How does a ghost start a letter?
"Tomb it may concern."

~~~~~~~~~~~~~~~~~

What is the favorite game at a ghost's Halloween party?
Hide and Shriek.

~~~~~~~~~~~~~~~~~

Why is the ghouls' football pitch wet?
Because players keep dribbling on it.

~~~~~~~~~~~~~~~~~

What's big and read and lies upside down in a gutter?
A dead bus.

What do young ghosts call their parents?
Deady and Mummy.

What do you call the spot in the middle of a graveyard?
The dead center.

What do ghosts use to phone home?
A terror-phone.

Where do ghoulies go to on the day before a Halloween party?
To the boo-ty parlor.

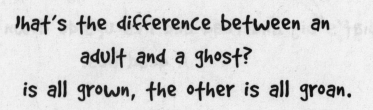

What's the difference between an adult and a ghost?
is all grown, the other is all groan.

Which are ghosts' favorite days of the week?
Moan-day and fright-day.

What do you call a ghost's mistake?
A boo-boo.

Who did the ghost invite to his party?
Anyone he could dig up.

What's the difference between ghosts
and patched jeans?
Ghosts are dead men. Patched jeans are men-ded.

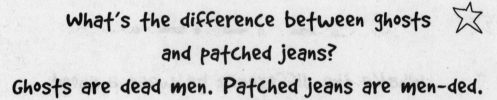

Why did the robot turn into a ghost?
Because he couldn't rust in peace.

What does a headless horseman ride?
A nightmare.

What did the headless horseman say when someone
gave him a comb?
"I will never part with this."

What's the difference between a ghost
and peanut butter?
A ghost doesn't stick to the roof of your mouth.

SKELETONS

Why didn't the skeleton go to the party?
He had no body to go with.

What happened when the skeletons rode pogo sticks?
They had a rattling good time.

Why did the skeleton go to hospital?
To have his ghoul stones removed.

How did the skeleton know it was going to rain?
He could feel it in his bones.

. . . . .

What's a skeleton's favorite musical instrument?
A from-bone.

. . . . .

If a skeleton rings your doorbell, is he a dead ringer?

. . . . . .

How does a skeleton call his friends?
On the telebone.

What do you call a skeleton that won't get up in the morning?
Lazy bones.

. . . . . .

What do boney people use to get into their houses?
Skeleton keys.

. . .

What do you call a skeleton who acts in Westerns?
Skint Eastwood.

. . . . . .

What happened to the boat that sank in the sea full of piranha fish?
It came back with a skeleton crew.

. . .

What do you call a skeleton snake?
A rattler.

. . . . . .

Which skeleton wore a kilt?
Boney Prince Charlie.

. . .

What is a skeleton's favorite drink?
Milk - it's so good for the bones.

Why did the skeleton stay out in the snow all night?
He was a numbskull.

What do you call a stupid skeleton?
Bonehead.

What happened to the skeleton who stayed by the fire all night?
He was bone dry.

What happened to the lazy skeleton?
He was bone idle.

What's the definition of a skeleton?
Bones with the person scraped off.

Why did the skeleton schoolgirl stay late at school?
She was boning up for her exams.

What sort of soup do skeletons like?
One with plenty of body in it.

What do you call a skeleton doctor?
Bones.

What happened to the skeleton who was
swallowed by a big fish?
He had a whale of a time.

What do you call the famous 18th-century
skeleton who was cremated?
Bone-ash (Beau Nash....geddit?)

Why did the skeleton run up a tree?
Because a dog was after its bones.

~~~~~~~~~~~~~~~~~~~~~~

How do you make a skeleton laugh?
Tickle his funny bone.

~~~~~~~~~~~~~~~~~~~~~~

Why did the bat miss the bus?
Because he hung around too long.

~~~~~~~~~~~~~~~~~~~~~~

Why do you have to wait so long for a ghost
train to come along?
They only run a skeleton service.

~~~~~~~~~~~~~~~~~~~~~~

What did the skeleton say to his girlfriend?
I love every bone in your body.

~~~~~~~~~~~~~~~~~~~~~~

Why wasn't the naughty skeleton
afraid of the police?
Because he knew they couldn't pin
anything on him.

How do skeletons get their
mail?
By Bony Express.

What happened to the
skeleton who went to a
party?
All the others hung their
coats on him.

Why don't skeletons play
music in church?
They have no organs.

What kind of plate does a
skeleton eat off?
Bone China.

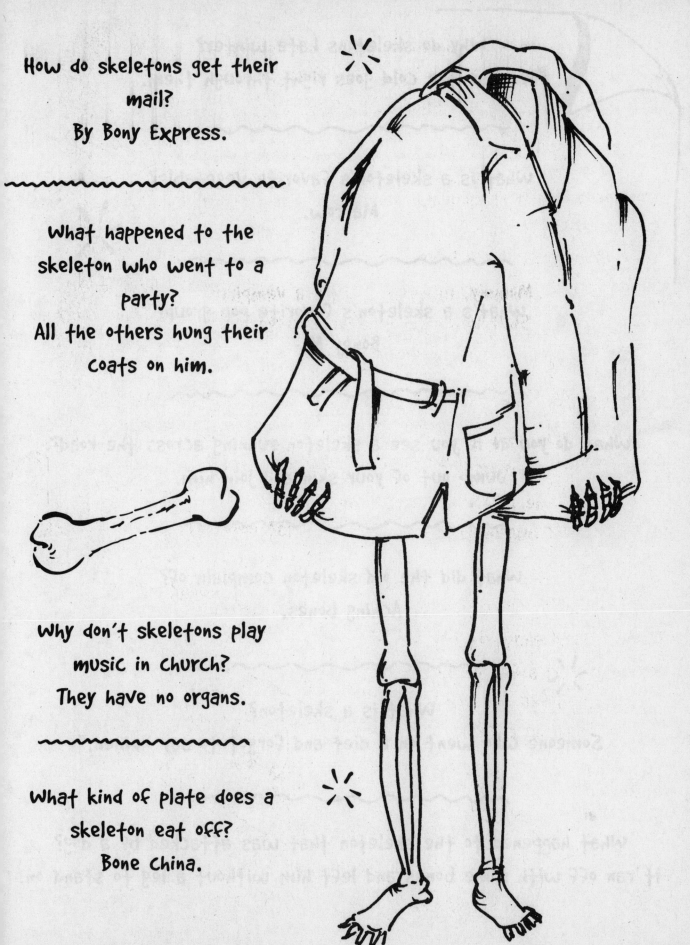

Why do skeletons hate winter?
Because the cold goes right through them.

What is a skeleton's favorite vegetable?
Marrow.

What's a skeleton's favorite pop group?
Boney M.

What do you do if you see a skeleton running across the road?
Jump out of your skin and join him.

What did the old skeleton complain of?
Aching bones.

What is a skeleton?
Someone who went on a diet and forgot to say "When."

What happened to the skeleton that was attacked by a dog?
It ran off with some bones and left him without a leg to stand on.

Why are skeletons so calm?
Nothing gets under their skin.

What do you call a skeleton that's always telling lies?
A boney phony.

Why didn't the skeleton want to go to school?
Because his heart wasn't in it.

VILLAINS

There's a plan to bring back hanging but only in London, Paris, Washington, and Tokyo.
It's for capital offenses.

What did everyone say about the kind-hearted pirate?
That his barque was worse than his bite.

— — —

What did the executioner say to his wife?
Only 30 chopping days to Christmas.

— — —

Which villains steal soap from the bath?
Robber ducks.

What does an executioner do with a pen and
paper?
Writes his chopping list.

Why was the actor pleased to be on the gallows?
Because at last he was in the noose.

Why was the robber so secure?
He was a safe robber.

Why was the robber bionic?
He was holding up a bank.

What did the robber say when he asked for some
glue and sticky tape?
"This is a stick-up!"

What's another word for a murderer who kills old
ladies?
A Killergran.

Why was Mac the Knife so amusing?
He had a very sharp wit.

What is the Guillotine?
A French chopping center.

What happened at the outlaws' party?
The chief outlaw's mother-in-law turned up because she
thought it was an in-laws party.

How do you survive the electric chair?
Insulate your underpants.

What happened when the man who was about to be shot was
offered a cigarette?
He refused it for reasons of health.

How did the villain try to get out of being hanged?
He said he never wore a tie.

Why was the villain on the gallows smiling?
He was knot-happy.

In Spain they use a garotte.
It's pretty g'rotty.

What do you call a highwayman who is ill?
Sick Turpin.

What happened when a very suspicious man
was taken to the gallows?
He said, "Is this a trap?"

~~~~~~~~~~~~~~~~~~~~~

Why was he hanged in the evening?
Because it was the six o'clock noose.

~~~~~~~~~~~~~~~~~~~~~

Why did the villain start thinking about the old times
when he was on the gallows?
He felt noose-talgic.

Why did the burglar steal a washing machine? He wanted to make a clean getaway.

WEREWOLVES

Mommy, mommy, what's a werewolf?
Shut up John and comb your face.

Why was the werewolf
arrested in the butcher's
shop?
He was chop-lifting.

◦ ▭ ◦ ▭ ◦

What parting gift did a
mommy werewolf give to
her son when he left home?
A comb.

What happened when the werewolf fell in the washing machine?
He became a wash-and-werewolf.

◦ ▭ ◦ ▭ ◦

What happened to the werewolf who ate garlic?
His bark was worse than his bite.

Who are some of the werewolves' cousins?
The whatwolves and the whenwolves.

Why did the small werewolf bite the woman's ankle?
Because he couldn't reach any higher.

What do you get if you cross a werewolf with a hyena?
I don't know but if it laughs I'll join in.

Where does a werewolf sit in the theater?
Anywhere he wants to!

What do you call a werewolf who drinks too much?
A whino.

What happened when the werewolf chewed a bone for an hour?
When he got up he only had three legs.

What do you get if you cross a werewolf with a frog?
A creature that can bite you from the other side of the road.

How do you know that a werewolf's been in the fridge?
There are paw prints in the butter.

🌀 🌀 🌀 🌀 🌀 🌀

How do you know that two werewolves have been in the fridge?
There are two sets of paw prints in the butter.

🌀 🌀 🌀 🌀 🌀 🌀

What does it mean if there is a werewolf in your fridge in the morning?
You had some party last night!

How do you stop a werewolf chasing you?
Throw a stick and say "fetch!"

^   x   x   x

What do you get if you cross a hairdresser with a werewolf?
A monster with an all-over perm.

^   x   x

What happened when the werewolf swallowed a clock?
He got ticks.

Why shouldn't you grab a werewolf by its tail?
It might be the werewolf's tail but it could be the end of you.

⋏ ✗ ✗

I used to be a werewolf but I'm all right noooooooooooooooooow!

⋏ ✗ ✗ ✗

Why are werewolves thought of as quick-witted?
Because they always give snappy answers.

⋏ ✗ ✗

Why did the mummy and daddy werewolves call their son camera?
Because he was always snapping.

⋏ ✗ ✗ ✗

What do you call a hairy beast with clothes on?
A wear-wolf.

⋏ ✗ ✗

How do you make a werewolf stew?
Keep him waiting for two hours.

⋏ ✗ ✗ ✗

Why did the boy take an aspirin after hearing a werewolf howl?
Because it gave him an eerie ache.

What do you call a hairy beast in a river?
A weir-wolf.

What do you call a hairy beast that no
longer exists?
A were-wolf.

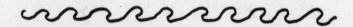

What do you call a hairy beast that's lost?
A where-wolf.

What happens if you cross a werewolf
with a sheep?
You have to get a new sheep.

What's fearsome, hairy and drinks from
the wrong side of a glass?
A werewolf with hiccoughs.

BOOK TITLES

Never Make a Witch Angry - by Sheila Tack

The Vampire's Victim - by E. Drew Blood

The Bad-Tempered Werewolf - by Claudia Armoff

Chased by a Werewolf - by Claude Bottom

The Omen - by B. Warned

Keeping Pet Snakes - by Sir Pent

Mysterious Murders - by Ivor Clue

Robbers Who Got Away With It - by Hugh Dunnit

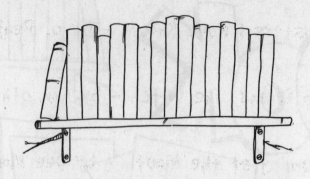

Ghost Stories - by I.M.Scared

Going on A Witch Hunt - by count Miout

I Saw a Witch in the Mirror - by Douglas cracked

The Greediest Monster in the World - by Buster Gutt

The Monster Hanging off the Cliff - by Alf Hall

The Hungry Yeti - by Aida Lot

When a Wizard Knocks on Your Door - by Wade Aminit

Don't Go Near Dracula - by Al Scream

Tracking Monsters - by Woody Hurt

I Met An Abominable Snowman - by Anne Tarctic

Monsters I Have Known - by O. Penjaw

My Best Friend, The Witch - by Ann otherwitch

Foaming at the Mouth - by Dee Monic

Wizard from Another Planet - by A. Lee-En

I saw a Witch - by Denise R. Knockin

In the Witch's Cauldron - by Mandy ceased

Boo! - by Terry fied

The Witch meets Dracula - by Pearce Nex

The Ghost of the Witch - by Eve L. Spirit

How to feed werewolves - by Nora Bone

Black Magic – by Sue Pernatural

Witch's Coven – by De Ville Worshiper

Terrible Spells – by B .Witcher.

Collecting Reptiles – by Ivor Frog

How to be a Witch – by Ruth Less

Swallowing Dr Jekyll's Potion – by Iris Keverything

I Saw a Vampire – by Ron Fast

A Ghost in My House – by Olive N. Fear

Collecting Mosquitoes – by Lara Bites

How to Escape from a Witch – by Shelby Lucky

How to Keep Vampires from Your House – by Dora Steel

Make Money from Rich Wizards – by Marie Mee

Collecting Mosquitoes – by Ethan Alive

When to go Monster-Hunting – by Mae B. Tomorrow.

A Houseful of Ghouls – by Roxie Horror

Bungee Jumping with Monsters – by Wade R. Go

A Wizard's Biography – by Eli D. Constantly

A Very Hungry Giant – by Ethan D. Lot

Escape from the Vampire – by Jess N. Time

I Caught the Loch Ness Monster – by Janet A. Big-Wun

In My Crystal Ball – by Thea Lot

Collecting Wriggly Creatures – by Tina Worms

How I Became a Werewolf – by Olive Alone

Catching Villains – by Laura Norder

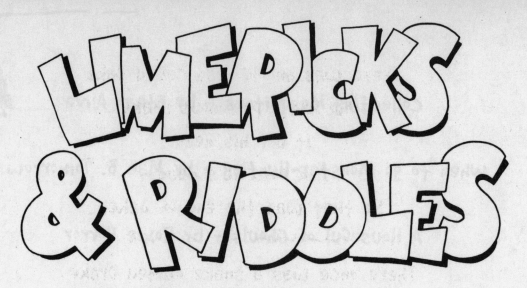

LIMERICKS & RIDDLES

While visiting close friends, a gnat,
Decided to sleep in a hat
But an elderly guest
Decided to rest
Now the gnat and the hat are quite flat.

~~~~~~~~~~~~~~~~~

There once was a very strong cat
Who had a fight with a bat
The bat flew away
And at the end of the day
The cat had a scrap with a rat.

~~~~~~~~~~~~~~~~~

A cobra was invited to dine
By his charmingly cute valentine
But when he got there
He found that the fare
Was pineapple dumplings with wine.

There was an old man called Jake
Who had a poisonous snake
It bit his head
And now he's dead
So that was the end of Jake.

~~~~~~~~~~~~~~~~

There once was a snake named Drake
Who stared a fight with a rake
It cut off his tail
Drake went very pale
And that is the end of my tale.

There once was a lonely young jellyfish
Who then met a sweet, loving shellyfish.
They went with the motion
of waves in the ocean
And became better known as the jollyfish.

There was an old wizard from Brazil
Who always ate more than his fill
He thought it no matter
That his waistline grew fatter
But he burst. Does that not make you ill?

There was a big monster from Leek
Who, instead of a nose, had a beak.
It grew quite absurd
Till he looked like a bird.
He migrates at the end of the next week.

A boa with coils uneven
Had the greatest trouble in breathing
With jokes she was afflicted
For her laughs got constricted
And her coils started writhing and wreathing.

There was a young girl from Hyde
Who fell down a hole and died
Her unfortunate mother
Tripped up on another
And now they're interred side by side.

A witch and a wizard from Rye
Courted for years side by side.
He said, "Dear we've tarried,
Why don't we get married?"
"Cos no one would have us," she cried.

There was an old monster with humps
Who was terribly down in the dumps
He was frumpy and grumpy
And jumpy and stumpy
Because of his terrible lumps.

~~~~~~~~~~~~~~~

A cannibal known as Ned
Ate potato crisps in his bed.
His mother said, "Sonny
It's not very funny
Why don't you eat people instead?"

~~~~~~~~~~~~~~~

A fat witch who lived on the Rhine
Was asked at what hour she'd dine.
She said, "At seven,
And half past eleven,
With a snack at a quarter to nine."

~~~~~~~~~~~~~~~

There once was a man from Brazil,
Who of pumpkin ate more than his fill.
He thought it no matter
That he grew fatter
But he burst – which makes me quite ill.

A fly and a flea in a flue
Were wondering what they should do.
Said the fly, "Let us flee!"
Said the flea, "Let us fly!"
So they flew, through a flaw in the flue.

~~~~~~~~~~

There was a young yeti from Gloucester
Whose granny and grandfather lost 'er.
Next day she was found
In the snow-covered ground
But they didn't know how to defrost her.

~~~~~~~~~~

There was a young cannibal from Kew
Whose girlfriend said "I'll be true,
But please understand
That along with my hand
The rest of me comes with it, too."

~~~~~~~~~~

A wizard who's bald as a bat
Spilt hair tonic over the mat.
It's grown so much higher
He can't see the fire
And he thinks that it's smothered his cat.

There was a big monster called Ned
Who had eyes at the back of his head.
When asked where he's going,
"I've no way of knowing.
But I know where I've been to," he said.

There was a young witch from Nantes
Who hated each one of her aunts.
So she buried the lot
In her vegetable plot
And grew some remarkable plants.

It is a terrible night and Greg the Ghoul is out playing in it.
There's thunder and lightning and all the graves are opening
and all the nasty things that ever there were are
wandering the earth.
Question: What did Greg's mother say?
Answer: "Come in Greg."

Greg comes in. He says, "Mum, I've had a terrible time. For
a start this vampire bit me on the neck. Then after that
this werewolf chased me all round the graveyard. Then, as I
was coming home, all kinds of ghouls tried to trap me and
I've bruised my leg."
Question: What did Greg's mother say?
Answer: "You're going to a different playgroup."

ALIENS

What did the alien say when his flying saucer landed in a stud farm?
"Take me to your breeder!"

What do Scully and Moulder look into in December?
The X-mas files.

What do you call a starship full of wizards?
Flying sorcery.

What do you call an alien starship that drips water?
A crying saucer.

How did the aliens hurt the farmer?
They trod on his corn.

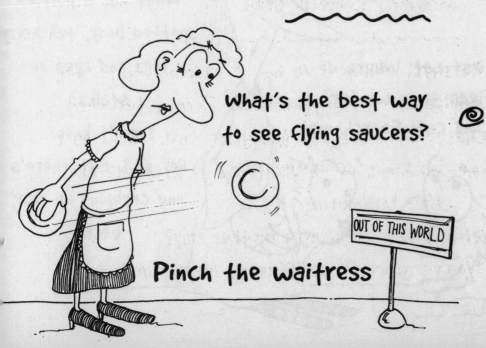

What's the best way to see flying saucers?

Pinch the waitress

OUT OF THIS WORLD

Why was the restaurant called "out of this world"?
Because it was full of Unidentified Frying objects.

I SAY, I SAY, I SAY

1st Cannibal: My wife's a tough old bird.

2nd Cannibal: You should have left her in the oven for another half an hour.

1st person: I've just been bitten by a snake on one arm.

2nd person: Which one?

1st person: I don't know, one snake looks very much like the next one.

First cat: Where do fleas go in winter?
Second cat: Search me!

What has a purple-spotted body, ten hairy legs and eyes on stalks?
I don't know.
Nor do I, but there's one creeping up your back!

1st bat: Fancy going out for a bite tonight?

2nd bat: No. I think I'll just hang around.

———

Visitor: Wow, you have a lot of flies buzzing round your horses and cows. Do you ever shoo them?

Rancher: No, we just let them go barefoot.

———

Girl: Can you eat spiders?

Boy: Why?

Girl: One's just crawled into your sandwich.

———

Mommy monster: What are you doing with that saw and where's your little brother?

Young monster: Hee, hee, he's my half-brother now.

~~~~~~

1st cannibal: I don't know what to make of my husband these days.

2nd cannibal: How about a curry?

1st man: I can trace my ancestors back to royalty.

2nd man: Yeh, right – to King Kong!

Boy: Mom, mom, I've just swallowed a spider.
Mom: Shall I get the doctor to give you something for it?
Boy: No, let it starve to death.

Mommy, mommy, why can't we have
a garbage bin like everyone else?
Shut up and keep chewing.

Mommy monster: Did you catch everyone's eyes
in that dress dear?
Girl monster: Yes, mum, and I've brought them
all home for cedric to play marbles with.

Bluebottle: I must fly.
Bee: ok, I'll give you a
buzz later.

1st vampire: Are you a light sleeper?
2nd vampire: No, I sleep in the dark.

Mother: John, why did you put a slug in
auntie's bed?
John: Because I couldn't find a snake.

o   o

1st monster: I've just changed my mind.
2nd monster: Does it work any better?

o   o

Girl: We had Auntie Mabel for lunch
last Sunday.
Boy: Really? We had roast beef.

o   o

Little monster: Mom I've
finished. Can I leave the table?
Mommy monster: Yes, I'll save it
for your tea.

o   o

Boy: Mom, why can't I swim in Loch Ness?
Mother: Because there are monsters in it.
Boy: But Daddy's swimming
there.
Mother: That's different.
He's insured.

Mommy, mommy, what's a vampire?
Shut up and drink your tomato juice
before it clots.

Witch: Men keep telling
me I'm beautiful.
Wizard: Some people have
very vivid imaginations.

1st monster: I have a hunch.
2nd monster: I thought you were a
funny shape.

Mother: Keep that dog out of the
house, it's full of fleas.
Son: Keep out of the house, Fido,
it's full of fleas.

Witch: When I'm old and ugly will you still love me.
Wizard: I do now, don't I?

Witch: Will I lose my looks as I get older?
Wizard: With luck, yes.

Boy: My sister's the school swot.
Girl: Does she do well in exams?
Boy: No, but she kills a lot of flies.

◇ ◇

Boy: Dad, Dad, there's a spider in the bath.
Dad: What's wrong with that? You've seen spiders before.
Boy: Yes, but this one is three feet wide and using all the hot water!

◇ ◇

Boy: Grandad, do you know how to croak?
Grandad: No, I don't think so. Why?
Boy: Because Daddy says he'll be a rich man when you do.

◇ ◇

Wizard: You remind me of the sea.
Witch: Why? Because I'm wild, free and romantic?
Wizard: No, because you make me sick.

1st zombie: Do you still hold your
girlfriend's hand?
2nd zombie: Yes, but I wish the rest of
her would visit more often.

1st Cannibal: Your son's very full
of himself isn't he?
2nd Cannibal: Yes, that's because
he bites his nails.

1st monster: My Dad's teaching me how to play squash.
2nd monster: Yeah? How is he doing that?
1st monster: He keeps pushing me into a telephone box.

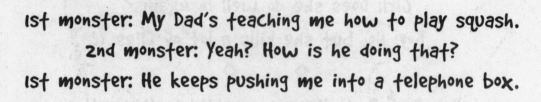

Mommy monster: Agatha, how often must I tell you
not to eat with your fingers.
Agatha monster: Sorry mom.
Mommy monster: I should think so! Use a shovel like I do.

Barber: Did you come in

with a red scarf on?

Wizard: No.

Barber: oh dear, I must

have cut your throat.

1st vampire: I live on garlic alone.

2nd vampire: Anyone who does that should live alone.

~~~~~~

1st man: My wife eats like a bird.

2nd man: You mean she hardly eats a thing?

1st man: No, she eats slugs and worms.

~~~~~~

1st Cannibal: We had burglars last night.

2nd Cannibal: Did they taste good?

– – · – ·

1st snake: I'm glad I'm not poisonous!

2nd snake: Why?

1st snake: Because I've just bitten my tongue.

Witch: Officer, you must help. I've just lost my wig.

Policeman: Certainly madam, we'll comb the area.

Girl: My dad wants to destroy his flea circus.

Boy: What do the fleas think about that?

Girl: They're hopping mad.

Boy: Where do fleas go in the winter?

Girl: Search me!

Witch: Eat your spinach – it'll put color in your cheeks.

Little witch: I don't want green cheeks!

Wizard: Have you put the cat out?

Witch: Was he burning again?

1st man: I've just been stung
by a bee.
2nd man: How was that?
1st man: I was charged $10
for a pot of honey.

1st witch: See my cat? He's just drunk 83 saucers of milk.
2nd witch: That must be a lap record.

Girl: Do you know which family the octopus belongs to?
Boy: No one in our street.

1st monster: I was in the zoo last week.
2nd monster: Really, which cage were you in?

1st apple: You look down in the dumps. What's eating you?
2nd apple: Worms I think.

1st monster: That pretty girl over there just rolled her eyes at me.
2nd monster: Well you'd better roll them back to her, she might need them.

Boy: Do you like monsters?
Girl: Sometimes.
Boy: How do you mean?
Girl: The times when they're away.

Boy: What's the biggest ant in the world?
Girl: My Aunt Fatima.
Boy: No, it's an elephant.
Girl: You obviously haven't met my Aunt Fatima.

Barber: Oops! Sorry, I've just cut your chin.
Vampire: Don't worry, it's not my blood.

Witch: Why do you keep losing your temper?
Wizard: Because it's all the rage!

1st Witch: How do you manage to make so many bad spells in one day?
2nd Witch: I get up early.

I'm not fishing, I'm drowning worms.

1st ghoul: You don't look too well today.

2nd ghoul: No, I'm dead on my feet.

1st Cannibal: Come and have dinner in our hut tonight.

2nd Cannibal: What are you having?

1st Cannibal: Hard-boiled legs.

1st Cannibal: I can't find anything to eat!

2nd Cannibal: But the jungle's full of people.

1st Cannibal: Yes but they're all very unsavory.

What are you fishing for sonny?

Young vampire: Dad, Dad, I know what you're getting for your birthday.

Vampire: Really, how?

Young vampire: I felt your presence.

Joe: Did you ever see a horse fly?
Pete: No, but I once saw a cow jump off a cliff.

Witch: Why have you stopped playing cards with my sister?
Wizard: Well, would you play with someone who cheats
all the time, is a poor loser and keeps tearing up
the cards?
Witch: No, I wouldn't.
Wizard: No, well nor will she.

Boy: Dad, Dad, come out. My sister's fighting
this ten foot gargoyle with three heads.
Dad: No, I'm not coming out. He's going to
have to learn to look after himself.

Wizard: You have
the face of a
saint.
Witch: Really,
which one?
Wizard: A Saint
Bernard.

1st monster: Who was that lady
I saw you with last night?
2nd monster: That was no lady,
that was my lunch.

Jailer: Come on, son, you're in for the chop.
Convicted killer: Oh no! I ordered steak and fries.

Boy: Dad, Dad, there's a three-headed policeman outside.
Dad: What did he say?
Boy: Hello, hello, hello.

1st man: Did you know that the headless horseman's gone to the looney bin?

2nd man: No, why's that?

1st man: Well, he's not all there.

◇   ◇

Boy: I once met a lion who had been bitten by a snake.
Girl: What did he say?
Boy: Nothing, silly, lions don't talk!

Mom, mom, a monster's just bitten my foot off.

Well keep out of the kitchen, I've just washed the floor.

Cannibal: Mom, mom, I've been eating a missionary and I feel sick.
Mom: Well, you know what they say - you can't keep a good man down.

Surveyor: This house is a ruin. I wonder what
stops it from falling down.
owner: I think the woodworm are holding hands.

Boy: What's black, slimy, has hairy legs and eyes on stalks?
Mom: Eat the cookies and don't worry what's in the tin.

old Witch: I know you want a job with me. Do you tell lies?
Young Witch: No, but I can pick it up.

Boy: Did you know you can get fur from a three-headed mountain monster?
Girl: Really, what kind of fur?
Boy: As fur away as possible!

Little monster: Mom, mom, what's for tea?
Mother monster: Shut up and get back in the microwave.

Baby ghost: Please, mom, tell me some more stories about the old haunted house.
Mother ghost: I can't dear, its a one-story house.

1st Cannibal: I don't know what to make of my husband.
2nd Cannibal: How about a hotpot?

Witch: What day is it?
Wizard: Halloween.
Witch: Yes, hello to you too, Ivan, but what day is it?

Boy: A vampire told me a joke yesterday.

Girl: Was it good?

Boy: It was a scream.

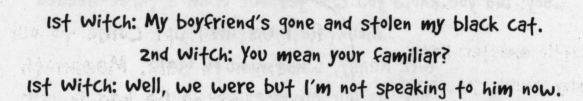

1st Witch: My boyfriend's gone and stolen my black cat.

2nd Witch: You mean your familiar?

1st Witch: Well, we were but I'm not speaking to him now.

Boy scout: I'm in agony. I've been stung by a bee.

Scout leader: Well, we'll put some cream on it.

Boy scout: You'll be lucky, it must be miles away by now.

Witch: I want you to come round the world with
me on a broomstick.

Wizard: Are you taking me for a ride?

Sergeant: Constable, I want you to stand guard
outside the graveyard tonight.

Constable: But what do I do if I see some body-snatchers?

Sergeant: Just keep calm and don't get carried away.

1st witch: I'm so unlucky.

2nd witch: Why?

1st witch: Last night I went to a party and met a handsome
prince.

2nd witch: What's unlucky about that?

1st witch: When I kissed him he turned into a frog.

Father: Why did you put a toad in your sister's bed?
Son: I couldn't find a spider.

The police are looking for a monster with one eye.
Why don't they use two?

Little monster: Daddy, Daddy, you've got carrots sprouting out of your ears.
Big monster: That's funny, I planted radishes.

Roll up, roll up! Come to our mammoth sale. Mammoth bargains to be had in our mammoth sale.

Don't be silly! No one round here's got room in their houses for a mammoth.

1st werewolf: A vampire bit me on the neck last night.
2nd werewolf: Did you put anything on it?
1st werewolf: No, it seemed to like it as it was.

1st boy: Are you having a party for your birthday?
2nd boy: No, I'm having a witch do.
1st boy: What's a witch do?
2nd boy: She flies around on a broomstick casting spells.

What would you do if you saw a big, horrible monster?

Hope that he hadn't seen me too.

1st boy: My Dad saw a horrible witch and didn't turn a hair!
2nd boy: I'm not surprised – your Dad's bald!

1st Witch: I spend hours in front of a mirror admiring my beauty. Do you think that's vanity?

2nd Witch: No, it's imagination.

✗   ✗

Witch: I have the face of a 16-year-old girl.

Wizard: Well you'd better give it back, you're making it all wrinkly.

✗   ✗

1st Witch: What's your new boyfriend like?

2nd Witch: He's mean, nasty, ugly, smelly and totally evil — has some bad points too.

Teacher: What did Robert the Bruce do after watching the spider climbing up and down?

Pupil: He went and invented the yo-yo.

✓   ✓

1st Witch: (Before a cricket match) How do you hold a bat?

2nd Witch: By the wings of course!

✓   ✓

1st Witch: My beauty is timeless.

2nd Witch: Yes, it could stop a clock.

Witch: Have you ever seen someone
who looked like me before?
Girl: Yes, but I had to pay
admission.

———

Young witch: Daddy, I'm so glad
you called me Godzilla.
Wizard: Why?
Young witch: Because that's what
the kids call me at school.

———

Wizard: What's the matter son?
Young wizard: The boy next door says I look just like you?
Wizard: What did you say?
Young wizard: Nothing, he's bigger than me.

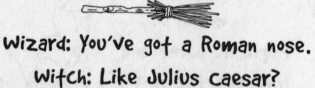

Wizard: You've got a Roman nose.
Witch: Like Julius Caesar?
Wizard: No, it's roamin' all over your face.

———

1st monster: What is that son of yours doing these days?
2nd monster: He's at medical school.
1st monster: Oh, what's he studying?
2nd monster: Nothing, they're studying him.

1st Witch: I took my son to the zoo yesterday.

2nd Witch: Really, did they accept him?

1st Witch: I'm going to France tomorrow.

2nd Witch: Are you going by broom?

1st Witch: No, by hoovercraft.

1st Wizard: I don't think much of your toad.

2nd Wizard: Never mind, eat the vegetables instead.

1st Witch: I went to the beauty parlor yesterday. I was there for three hours.

2nd Witch: Oh, what did you have done?

1st Witch: Nothing, I was just going in for an estimate.

Witch: I'd like some tiles for my bathroom.

Shopkeeper: But this is a pet shop.

Witch: That's all right – I want reptiles.

Witch: I'm looking for something to make my rock cakes light.

Shopkeeper: Sorry madam, we don't sell gasoline here.

1st Witch: Your little daughter's grown!

2nd Witch: Yes, she's gruesome.

Witch: You should keep control of your little boy. He just bit me on the ankle.

Vampire: That's only because he couldn't reach your neck.

1st Witch: Have you tried one of those new paper cauldrons?

2nd Witch: Yes.

1st Witch: Did it work?

2nd Witch: No, it was tearable.

1st Witch: Shall I buy black or blue candles?

2nd Witch: Which one burns longer?

1st Witch: Neither, they both burn shorter.

What goes "croak, croak"
when it's foggy?
A frog-horn.

—

1st Witch: Why do you keep throwing
bunches of garlic out of the window?
2nd Witch: To keep the vampires away.
1st Witch: But there aren't any
vampires round here.
2nd Witch: See, it works doesn't it!

1st Witch: I'm going to cast a spell
and make myself beautiful. I'll have
hundreds of men at my feet.
2nd Witch: Yes, chiropodists.

—

Child: Trick or treat.
Neighbor: Here are some sweets for you and some for your brother.
Child: Don't worry, you can have him without the sweets.

Boy: I bet I can get you to
forget the vampire.
Girl: What vampire?
Boy: See, you've forgotten him already.

———

Monster teacher: If I had two people beside me and
you had two people beside you, what would we have?
Monster: Lunch!

———

Witch: How much are your black candles?
Shopkeeper: Two dollars each.
Witch: That's candleous!

———

Mommy monster: Don't eat that uranium.
Little monster: Why not?
Mommy monster: You'll get atomic-ache.

———

Mrs Monster: Try to be nice to mother
when she comes to stay this weekend dear.
Mr Monster: How can I do that?
Mrs Monster: Well, fall down when
she hits you.

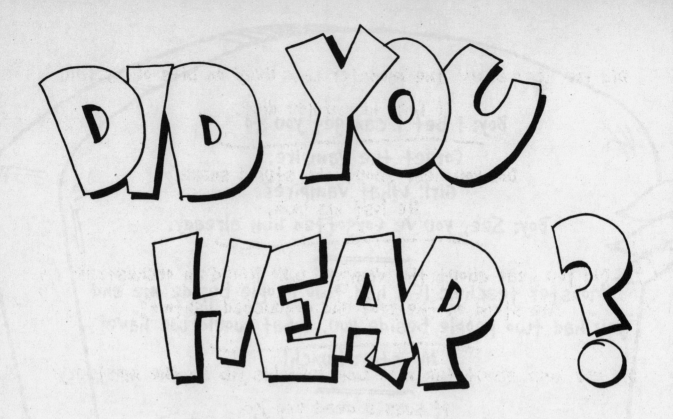

DID YOU HEAP?

Did you hear about the vampire who got married?
He proposed to his girl-fiend.

Did you hear the joke about the fierce yeti?
It'll make you roar.

Did you hear about the stupid wizard?
He couldn't remember if he used to be forgetful.

Did you hear the joke about the two monsters who crashed?
They fell off a cliff, boom, boom.

Did you hear about the vampire bicycle
that went round biting people's arms off?
It was a vicious cycle.

Did you hear about the monster who lived on bits of metal?
It was his staple diet.

Did you hear about the stupid snake?
He lost his skin.

Did you hear about the vampire who joined an orchestra?
He stood on the roof and conducted lightning.

Did you hear about the man who left his job at the mortuary?
It was a dead end job.

Did you hear about the stupid man who
walked into a crematorium
and asked "What's cooking?"

Did you hear about the monster who sent his picture to a
lonely hearts club?
They sent it back saying they weren't that lonely!

Did you hear about the man who believed in reincarnation?
In his will he left his money to himself.

Did you hear about the man who jumped in the Hudson River?
He committed sewercide.

Did you hear about the witch who met the
wizard in a revolving door?
They've been going round together ever since.

Did you hear about the vampire that was seen
crawling through the desert crying "Blood, blood."

Did you hear about the vampire who had an eye for the ladies?
He used to keep it in his pocket.

━ ━ ━

Did you hear about the man who tried to cross the
Loch Ness Monster with a goat?
He had to get a new goat.

━ ━ ━

Did you hear about the cannibals who captured a scrawny old hunter?
It gave them something to chew over.

Did you hear about the cannibal family who were caught
spying by the witchdoctor?
They were given a right roasting.

━ ━ ━

Did you hear about the cannibal who commited suicide?
He got himself into a terrible stew.

Did you hear about the comedian who entertained at a werewolves' party?
He had them howling in the aisles.

Did you hear about the headless horseman who
got a job in a department store?
He's the head buyer.

Did you hear about the ghost comedian?
He was booed off stage.

Did you hear about the skeleton who
couldn't jump out of the plane?
He had no guts.

Did you hear about the man in the electric chair who asked the
executioner to reverse the charges?

Did you hear about the considerate hangman?
He said, "Now, is the noose too tight?"

 Did you hear about the musical ghost?
He wrote haunting melodies.

Did you hear about the skeleton who wore a kilt?
He was called Boney Prince Charlie.

Did you hear about the monster who lost all his hair in the war?
He lost it in a hair raid.

Did you hear about the ghost who learnt to fly?
He was pleased to be back on terror-firma.

Did you hear about the wizard who turned his friend into an egg?
He kept trying to poach his ideas.

∽ ∽ ∽ ∽ ∽

Did you hear about the witch who kept turning her dog into milk?
She liked her daily pointa.

∽ ∽ ∽ ∽ ∽

Did you hear about the witch who invented a magic lift?
It's called a "spell-e-vator."

∽ ∽ ∽ ∽ ∽

Did you hear about the two men who were cremated at the same time?
It was a dead heat.

∽ ∽ ∽ ∽ ∽

Did you hear about the monster who had eight arms?
He said they came in handy.

Did you hear about the ghostly model who got into magazines?
She was a cover ghoul!

Did you hear about the ghost who wore glasses?
They were spooktacles.

Did you hear about the Italian ghost?
He liked spooketti.

Did you hear about the cannibal who went vegetarian?
He couldn't stop eating swedes.

Why did the cannibal go on a vegetarian diet?
He went off people.

Did you hear about the man who thought he was Dracula?
He was a pain in the neck.

―――――――――――

Did you hear about the smuggler who saw a ghost?
It was a ghostguard.

―――――――――――

Did you hear about the boy who saw a witch riding on a broomstick?
He said, "What are you doing on that?"
She replied, "My sister's got the vacuum cleaner."

―――――――――――

Did you hear about the monster who had an extra pair of hands?
Where did he keep them?
In a handbag.

―――――――――――

Did you hear about the sick ghost?
He had oooooo-ping cough.

Did you hear about the cannibal
who joined the police force?
He said he wanted to grill his suspects.

ʌ   x   x   x

Did you hear about the monster
who had twelve arms and no legs?
He was all fingers and thumbs.

ʌ   x   x   x

Did you hear about the
witch's child who was so ugly
they hired an actress to play
her in their home movies?

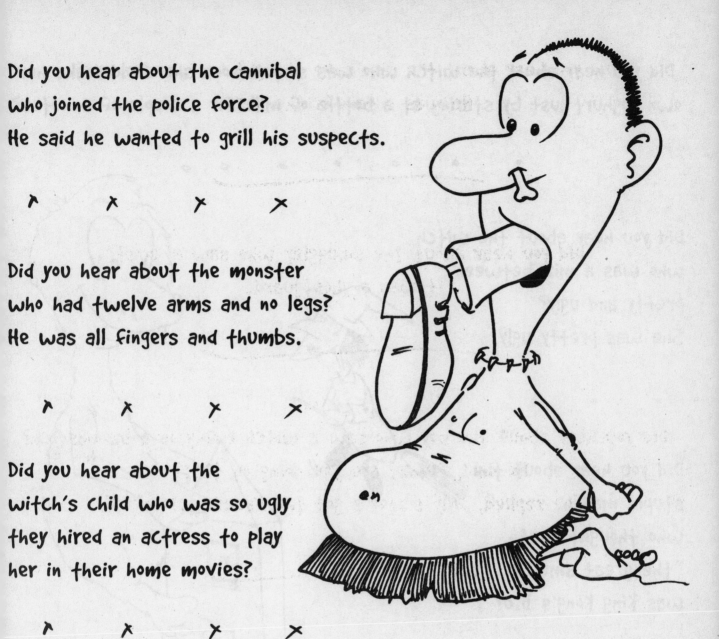

ʌ   x   x   x

Did you hear about the man who took up monster-baiting for a living?
He used to be a teacher but he lost his nerve.

ʌ   x   x   x

Did you hear about the witch who was so ugly that when a tear rolls
down her cheek it takes one look at her face and rolls straight up again?

Did you hear about the witch who was so poisonous she could make her own yoghurt just by staring at a bottle of milk for a couple of minutes?

• • • • • • • •

Did you hear about the witch
who was a mix between
pretty and ugly?
She was pretty ugly.

• • •

Did you hear about the
stupid man
who thought that
"the great smell of Brut"
was King Kong's B.o?

• • •

Did you hear about the witch who was ashamed of her long black hair?
She always wore long gloves to cover it up.

• • • • • •

Did you hear about the witch who did a four-year course in ugliness?
She finished it in two.

Did you hear about the witch who went in for the
"lovely legs" competition?
She was beaten by the microphone stand.

Did you hear about the wizard who can sculpt lots of
things out of skull bones?
Apparently he has a high degree of witchcraftsmanship.

✓   ✓   ✓   ✓

Did you hear about the witch who went on a crash diet?
She wrecked three cars and her broomstick.

✓   ✓   ✓   ✓

Did you hear about the very well behaved little wizard?
When he was good his father would give him a dime and a pat on the
head. By the time he was sixteen he had $50 and a totally flat head.

✓   ✓   ✓   ✓

Did you hear about the sick werewolf?
He lost his voice but it's howl right now.

Did you hear about the stupid jellyfish?
It set!

Did you hear about the man who set up a flea circus?
He started it from scratch.

Did you hear about the stupid woodworm?
He was found in a brick.

Did you hear about the vampire who died of a broken heart?
He had loved in vein.

Did you hear about the skeleton who challenged another to a duel?
It was called off as neither had the guts
to go through with it.

Did you hear about the glow-worm that
didn't know if it was coming or glowing?

Did you hear about the maggot that was shut up
in Tutankhamen's Tomb?
It had a phar-old time.

Did you hear about the flea who failed his exams?
He didn't come up to scratch.

Did you hear about the customer who complained about her mothballs?
She said she hadn't hit a single one with them!

Did you hear about the religious moth?
He gave up woollens for lint.

Did you hear about the woodworm who stopped doing his work?
He said it was boring.

Did you hear about the beautiful ancient Greek termite that lunched a thousand ships?

Did you hear about the boy who wanted to run away to the circus?
He ended up in a flea circus.

Did you hear about the witch who looked in the mirror?
It was a shattering experience.

UN-BREAKABLE MIRRORS

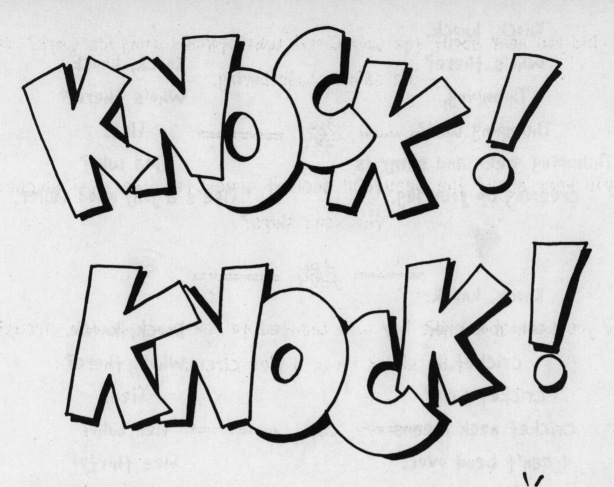

Knock, knock.
Who's there?
owl.
owl who?
owl I can say is knock knock!

Knock, knock.
Who's there?
owl.
owl who?
owl aboard!

Knock, knock.
Who's there?
owl.
owl who?
owl be sad if you don't
let me in.

Knock, knock.
Who's there?
Thumping.
Thumping who?
Thumping green and slimy is
creeping up your leg.

Knock, knock.
Who's there?
Cricket.
Cricket who?
Cricket neck means
I can't bend over.

Knock, knock.
Who's there?
Eel.
Eel who?
Eel meet again.

Knock, knock.
Who's there?
Weevil.
Weevil who?
Weevil work it out.

Knock, knock.
Who's there?
Flea.
Flea who?
Flea's a jolly good feller.

Knock, knock.
Who's there?
Flea.
Flea who?
Flea thirty!

Knock, knock.
Who's there?
Spider.
Spider who?
Spider through the keyhole.

328

Knock, knock.
Who's there?
Webster.
Webster who?
Webster Spin, your friendly neighborhood spider.

Knock, knock.
Who's there?
Mosquito.
Mosquito who?
Mosquito smoking soon.

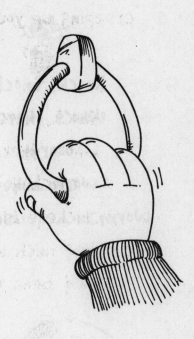

Knock, knock.
Who's there?
Fly.
Fly who?
Fly away soon.

Knock, knock.
Who's there?
Moth.
Moth who?
Moth people know the anthwer.

Knock, knock.
Who's there?
Earwig.
Earwig who?
Earwig come!

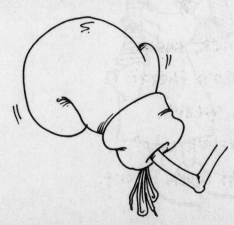

Knock, knock.
Who's there?
Grub.
Grub who?
Grub hold of my hand and let's go!

Knock, knock.
Who's there?
Worm.
Worm who?
Worm in here isn't it?

Knock, knock.
Who's there?
Bee.
Bee who?
Bee careful out there!

Knock, knock.
Who's there?
Roach.
Roach who?
Roach out and touch somebody.

Knock, knock.
Who's there?
Termite.
Termite who?
Termite's the night!

Knock, knock.
Who's there?
Army Ant.
Army Ant who?
Army Ants coming for tea then?

Knock, knock.
Who's there?
Wizard.
Wizard who?
Wizard you I'm lost.

Knock, knock.
Who's there?
Larva.
Larva who?
Larva cup of coffee.

Knock, knock.
Who's there?
Witch.
Witch who?
Witch witch would you like it to be?

Knock, knock.
Who's there?
Amos.
Amos who?
Amosquito.

Knock, knock.
Who's there?
Monster.
Monster who?
Monster munch.

Knock, knock.
Who's there?
Anna.
Anna who?
Annather mosquito.

Knock, knock.
Who's there?
Ben.
Ben who?
Ben Dover, the flexible cockroach.

Knock, knock.
Who's there?
King Kong.
King Kong who?
King Kong's now part of China.

Knock, knock.
Who's there?
Insect.
Insect who?
Insect your name and address here.

Knock, knock.
Who's there?
Ivy.
Ivy who?
Ivy cast a spell on you.

Knock, knock.
Who's there?
Bug.
Bug who?
Bugsy Malone

Knock, knock.
Who's there?
Ghost.
Ghost who?
Ghost town.

Knock, knock.
Who's there?
Ghoul.
Ghoul who?
Ghoulpost painter.

Knock, knock.
Who's there?
Fang.
Fang who?
Fangs for the memory.

Knock, knock.
Who's there?
Blood.
Blood who?
Blood brothers.

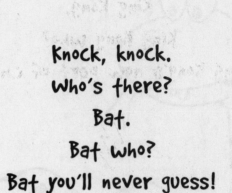

Knock, knock.
Who's there?
Bat.
Bat who?
Bat you'll never guess!

Knock, knock.
Who's there?
Bones.
Bones who?
Bones upon a time...

Knock, knock.
Who's there?
Snake.
Snake who?
Snake a move for it!

Knock, knock.
Who's there?
Coffin.
Coffin who?
Coffin and spluttering.

Knock, knock.
Who's there?
Adder.
Adder who?
Adder you get in here?

Knock, knock.
Who's there?
Viper.
Viper who?
Viper your nose!

Knock, knock.
Who's there?
Rattlesnake.
Rattlesnake who?
Rattlesnake a big difference!

Knock, knock.
Who's there?
Europe.
Europe who?
Europe early this morning, slimy.

Knock, knock.
Who's there?
Bernardette.
Bernardette who?
Bernardette all of my frogspawn fritters.

Knock, knock.
Who's there?
Baby owl.
Baby owl who?
Baby owl see you later, baby not.

Knock, knock.
Who's there?
Herman.
Herman who?
Herman Munster.

Knock, knock.
Who's there?
Turner.
Turner who?
Turner round, there's a monster
breathing down your neck.

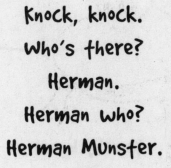

Knock, knock.
Who's there?
Woodworm.
Woodworm who?
Woodworm cake be enough or
would you like two?

Knock, knock.
Who's there?
Gus.
Gus who?
Gus what! There's a witch in the ditch!

Knock, knock.
Who's there?
Edwin.
Edwin who?
Edwin a spelling contest if I
were a better witch.

Knock, knock.
Who's there?
oliver.
oliver who?
oliver lone and I'm frightened
of monsters.

Knock, knock.
Who's there?
Jerome.
Jerome who?
Jerome alone through the woods
looking for victims.

Knock, knock.
Who's there?
Murphy.
Murphy who?
Murphy, have murphy! Don't
eat me!

Knock, knock.
Who's there?
Vic.
Vic who?
Victim of a vampire.

Knock, knock.
Who's there?
Harry.
Harry who?
Harry up! There's a ghoul
after us!

Knock, knock.
Who's there?
Tim.
Tim who?
Tim you got scared!

Knock, knock.
Who's there?
Barry.
Barry who?
Barry the dead.

Knock, knock.
Who's there?
Vincent.
Vincent who?
Vincent alive anymore.

337

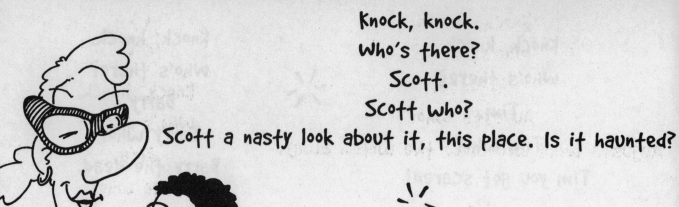

Knock, knock.
Who's there?
Scott.
Scott who?
Scott a nasty look about it, this place. Is it haunted?

Knock, knock.
Who's there?
Ellen.
Ellen who?
Ellen all the ghouls are after me.

Knock, knock.
Who's there?
Eunice.
Eunice who?
Eunice is a witch –
I thought you should know.

Knock, knock.
Who's there?
Cecile.
Cecile who?
Cecile th-the w-windows.
Th-there is a m-monster out there.

Knock, knock.
Who's there?
Arnold.
Arnold who?
Arnold man who looks like a wizard.

Knock, knock.
Who's there?
Augusta.
Augusta who?
Augusta wind will blow the witch away.

Knock, knock.
Who's there?
Enid.
Enid who?
Enid some shelter from the ghouls.

Knock, knock.
Who's there?
Thea.
Thea who?
Thea ghost.

Knock, knock.
Who's there?
Olive.
Olive who?
Olive in a haunted house.

Knock, knock.
Who's there?
Aida.
Aida who?
Aida whole village 'cos I'm a monster.

Knock, knock.
Who's there?
Jamie.
Jamie who?
Jamie'n you're a vampire.

Knock, knock.
Who's there?
Cliff.
Cliff who?
Cliffhanger.

Knock, knock.
Who's there?
Twyla.
Twyla who?
Twylight is when the vampires and
ghoulies come out to play.

Knock, knock.
Who's there?
Fido.
Fido who?
Fido known you were coming I'd
have bolted all the doors.

Knock, knock.
Who's there?
Marie.
Marie who?
Marie me or I'll cast a spell on you.

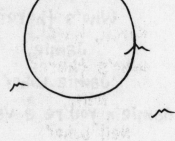

Knock, knock.
Who's there?
Dora.
Dora who?
Dora steel is needed to ward
off the nasty witches.

Knock, knock.
Who's there?
Adair.
Adair who?
Adair you to open this door and see
my fangs.

Knock, knock.

Who's there?

Max.

Max who?

Maximum security is needed
in these parts.

Knock, knock.

Who's there?

Jay.

Jay who?

Jaylbird with clanking chains.

Knock, knock.

Who's there?

Neil.

Neil who?

Neil down before the vampire king!

Knock, knock.

Who's there?

Doughnut.

Doughnut who?

Doughnut ask a dormouse silly
questions.

Knock, knock.

Who's there?

Dave.

Dave who?

Dave-andalised our home.

Knock, knock.
Who's there?
Reuben.
Reuben who?
Reuben my eyes 'cos I can't believe what
a big monster you are.

Knock, knock.
Who's there?
Crispin.
Crispin who?
Crispin crunchy frog sandwich.

Knock, knock.
Who's there?
Tristan.
Tristan who?
Tristan insect to really get up
your nose.

Knock, knock.
Who's there?
Mike.
Mike who?
Mike-andle's just blown out.
It's all dark.

Knock, knock.
Who's there?
Buster.
Buster who?
Buster blood vessel.

Knock, knock.
Who's there?
Alistair.
Alistair who?
Alistairs in this house creek
really spookily.

Knock, knock.
Who's there?
Paris.
Paris who?
Paris by the vampire very
quietly.

Knock, knock.
Who's there?
Mecca.
Mecca who?
Mecca run for it!

Knock, knock.
Who's there?
Glasgow.
Glasgow who?
Glasgow away from this place –
it's scary!

Knock, knock.
Who's there?
Kyoto.
Kyoto who?
Kyoto the priest before the
ghoulies get you.

Knock, knock.
Who's there?
Turin.
Turin who?
Turin to a werewolf under a full
moon.

Knock, knock.
Who's there?
Moscow.
Moscow who?
Moscow away from here.

Knock, knock.
Who's there?
Ghent.
Ghent who?
Ghent out of town.

Knock, knock.
Who's there?
Elsie.
Elsie who?
Elsie you later, alligator.

Knock, knock.
Who's there?
Haiti.
Haiti who?
Haiti-nything to do with witches!

Knock, knock.
Who's there?
Crete.
Crete who?
Crete to be safe at last.

Knock, knock.
Who's there?
Chile.
Chile who?
Chile being an abominable snowman!

Knock, knock.
Who's there?
Tehran.
Tehran who?
Tehran very slowly – there's a monster behind you.

Knock, knock.
Who's there?
Kenya.
Kenya who?
Kenya save me from the monsters?

Knock, knock.
Who's there?
Havana.
Havana who?
Havana spooky old time!

Knock, knock.
Who's there?
Congo.
Congo who?
Congo into the woods – it's dangerous.

Knock, knock.
Who's there?
Benin.
Benin who?
Benin hell.

Knock, knock.
Who's there?
Brighton.
Brighton who?
Brightonder the light of the full moon.

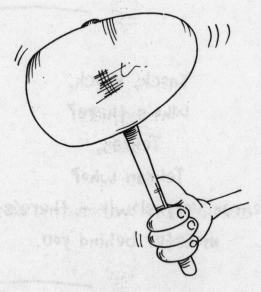

Knock, knock.
Who's there?
Dishes.
Dishes who?
Dishes the ant-force – open up.

Knock, knock.
Who's there?
Missouri.
Missouri who?
Missouri me! I'm so scared!

Knock, knock.
Who's there?
Russia.
Russia who?
Russiaway from this place – quick!.

Knock, knock.
Who's there?
Czech.
Czech who?
Czech before you open the door!

Knock, knock.
Who's there?
Rome.
Rome who?
Roming around looking for victims.

Knock, knock.
Who's there?
Ghana.
Ghana who?
Ghana get me a gun and shoot that werewolf.

Knock, knock.
Who's there?
Iran.
Iran who?
Iran all the way here. Let me in!

Doctor, doctor, I keep seeing an insect spinning round.
Don't worry, it's just a bug that's going round.

Monster: Doctor, doctor, how do I stop my nose from running?
Doctor: Stick out your foot and trip it up.

Witch: Doctor, my sisters think I'm mad because I like peas.
Doctor: There's nothing wrong with that, I like peas too.
Witch: Oh good, come back to my hovel and I'll show you my collection.

Doctor, doctor, I've got bad teeth, foul breath and smelly feet.
Sounds like you've got foot and mouth disease.

Wizard: Doctor, I'm having difficulty sleeping.
Doctor: Well maybe it's your bed.
Wizard: Oh, I'm all right at night, it's during the day I have problems.

Doctor, doctor, I think I'm turning into a frog.
Oh, you're just playing too much croquet.

Doctor: You need new glasses.
Monster: How did you guess?
Doctor: I could tell the moment you walked in through the window.

Patient: Doctor, doctor, I feel terrible. I can hardly breathe, I can't walk,
I keep having palpitations and my skin is covered in nasty blotches.
Doctor: Oh dear.
Patient: Are you writing me a prescription?
Doctor: No, a note for the undertaker.

Doctor: I'm sorry madam,
but I have to tell you are a
werewolf.
Patient: Right, give me a
piece of paper.
Doctor: Do you want to
write your will?
Patient: No, a list of people
I want to bite.

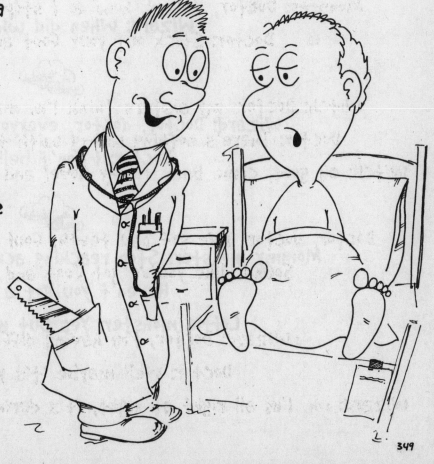

Doctor, doctor, I feel dead
from the waist down.
I'll arrange for you to be
half-buried.

349

Doctor, doctor, I'm so ugly. What can I do about it?
Hire yourself out for Hallowe'en parties.

Wizard: Doctor, doctor, I'm having trouble with my breathing.
Doctor: I'll give you something that will soon stop that.

Wizard: Doctor, doctor, I tend to flush a lot.
Doctor: Don't worry, that's just a chain reaction.

Wizard: Doctor, doctor, I think I'm losing my memory.
Doctor: When did this happen?
Wizard: When did what happen?

Wizard: Doctor, doctor, everyone thinks I'm a liar.
Doctor: I don't believe you.

Mommy monster: Stop reaching across the table like that.
Haven't you got a tongue?
Little monster: Yes but my arm's longer.

Witch: My new baby is the image of his father.
Doctor: Never mind. Just so long as he's healthy.

Monster: Doctor, doctor, what did the x-ray of my head show?
Doctor: Absolutely nothing.

Witch: Doctor, doctor, my baby's swallowed a bullet.
Doctor: Well don't point him at anyone until I get there.

Doctor: Don't worry about your health – you'll live until you're 80.
Wizard: I am 80.
Doctor: There, what did I tell you?

Monster: Doctor, doctor, I need to lose 30 pounds of excess flab.
Doctor: All right, I'll cut your head off.

Monster: Doctor, I think I'm a bridge.
Doctor: What on earth's come over you?
Monster: Six cars, two trucks and a bus.

Wizard: Doctor, I need something to keep my falling hair in.
Doctor: How about a matchbox?

Werewolf: Doctor, thank you so much for curing me.
Doctor: So you don't think you're a werewolf anymore?
Werewolf: Absolutely not. I'm quite clear now – see my nose is nice and cold.

Wizard: Doctor have you worked out what's the matter with me?
Doctor: I just don't know. It must be the drink.
Wizard: All right, I'll come back when you're sober.

~~~~~~~~~

Witch: I got up really early this morning and opened the door in my nightie!
Wizard: That's a funny place to keep a door.

Cannibal: Doctor, I keep thinking I'm a
slice of bread.
Doctor: You've got to stop loafing around.

Doctor, doctor, I keep thinking I'm a mosquito.
Go away, sucker.

────────〜〜〜〜〜〜〜〜〜〜〜〜〜〜〜〜────────

Doctor, doctor, I keep thinking I'm a moth.
So why did you come to see me?
Well, I saw the light in the window....

────────────────────

Doctor, doctor, I keep thinking I'm a python.
You can't get round me like that, you know.

353

Doctor, doctor, I keep thinking I'm an adder.
Good, could you help me with my tax return?

Monster: Doctor, doctor, I'm a blood-sucking monster and I keep needing to eat doctors.
Doctor: oh what a shame. I'm a dentist.

Vampire: Doctor, doctor, I keep thinking I'm a telephone.
Doctor: Why's that?
Vampire: I keep getting calls in the night.

Doctor, doctor, there's an invisible ghost in the waiting room.
Tell him I can't see him without an appointment.

Monster: Doctor, doctor, how long can one live without a brain?
Doctor: That depends. How old are you?

Witch: Doctor, doctor, I keep thinking I'm my own cat.
Doctor: How long have you thought this?
Witch: Since I was a kitten.

Frankenstein: Doctor, I'd like to leave my body to science.
Doctor: Don't bother. We couldn't find a cure for it.

Monster: Doctor, I have this irrepressible urge to paint myself all over in gold.
Doctor: Don't worry, it's just a gilt complex.

Doctor, I've just been bitten on the leg by a werewolf.
Did you put anything on it?
No, he seemed to like it as it was.

Doctor, doctor, I keep dreaming there are great, gooey, bug-eyed monsters playing tiddlywinks under my bed.
What shall I do?
Hide the tiddlywinks.

Doctor, doctor, I keep thinking I'm an invisible ghost.
Did someone say something?

~~~~~~~~~~

Witch: Doctor, doctor, each time I put my bra on I get thunder and lightning on my stomach.
Doctor: That's all right, it's just a storm in a C-cup.

~~~~~~~~~~

Doctor: Is your cough any better now?
Zombie: Yes, I've been coffin nicely for weeks, thank you.

~~~~~~~~~~

Wizard: Doctor, doctor, I keep thinking I'm a rubber band.
Doctor: Stretch yourself out on the couch.

~~~~~~~~~~

Monster: Doctor, I've got a split personality.
Doctor: Sit down, both of you.

~~~~~~~~~~

Wizard: Doctor, I snore so loudly I keep myself awake!
Doctor: Sleep in another room then.

~~~~~~~~~~

Witch: Doctor, doctor, my sister here keeps thinking she's invisible.
Doctor: Which sister?

Ghost: Doctor, I want to go on a diet.

Doctor: Why do you want to do that?

Ghost: Because I want to keep my ghoulish figure.

_ . _ . . _ . . _ .

Witch: I'm on a diet and it's making me irritable. Yesterday I bit someone's ear off!

Doctor: Oh dear, that's a lot of calories.

. _ _ . . _ . _ . _

Skeleton: Doctor, doctor, I keep thinking I'm a yo-yo.

Doctor: Are you stringing me along?

. _ . . _ . _

Doctor, doctor, I keep thinking you're a vampire. Necks please!

. _ . _ . _ . _

Doctor, doctor, I swallowed a skeleton's bone. Are you choking? No, I'm serious.

Doctor, doctor, every night I dream there are a thousand witches under my bed. What can I do?
Saw the legs off your bed.

Witch: Doctor, I've got a head like a turnip, three ears, two noses and a mouth the wrong way round. What am I?
Doctor: Ugly.

_____

Doctor, doctor, I keep thinking I'm a toad.
Go on, hop it!

_____

Doctor, doctor, I keep thinking I'm the Abominable Snowman.
Keep cool.

_____

Doctor: Did the mud pack help your appearance?
Monster: Yes, but it fell off after a few days.

Witch: Doctor, doctor, I don't feel well.

Doctor: Don't worry, you'll just have to go to bed for a spell.

Witch: Doctor, I can't help pulling ugly faces.

Doctor: Well there's nothing terrible about that.

Witch: There is when the people with the ugly faces don't like them being pulled!

Witch: Doctor, doctor, I keep dreaming of bats, creepy-crawlies, demons, ghosts, monsters, vampires, werewolves and yetis.

Doctor: How interesting. Do you always dream in alphabetical order?

Doctor, doctor, I keep thinking I'm a woodworm.
How boring.

Doctor, doctor, I keep thinking I'm a snake about to shed its skin.
Just slip into something more comfortable.

Doctor, doctor, I feel like an electric eel.
That's shocking.

Doctor, doctor, I keep thinking I'm a snail.
Don't worry, we'll soon have you out of your shell.

Doctor, doctor, I feel like an insignificant worm.
Next!

Doctor, doctor, I keep thinking I'm a nit.
Get out of my hair!

✹ ✹ ✹ ✹ ✹ ✹

Doctor, doctor, I keep thinking I'm a bee.
Buzz off!

✹ ✹ ✹ ✹ ✹ ✹

Doctor, doctor, I keep thinking I'm a frog.
What's wrong with that?
I think I'm going to croak.

✹ ✹ ✹ ✹ ✹ ✹

Doctor, doctor, I keep thinking I'm a butterfly?
Will you say what you mean and stop flitting about?

✹ ✹ ✹ ✹ ✹ ✹

Skeleton: Doctor, doctor, I feel like I've broken every bone.
Doctor: Well, be glad you're not a herring.

✹ ✹ ✹ ✹ ✹ ✹

Witch: Doctor, doctor, I've broken my arm in two places.
Doctor: Well, don't go back to those places again.

✹ ✹ ✹ ✹ ✹ ✹

Doctor, doctor, I keep thinking I'm a caterpillar.
Don't worry, you'll soon change.

✹ ✹ ✹ ✹ ✹ ✹

Doctor, doctor, I keep thinking I'm a spider.
What a web of lies!

✹ ✹ ✹ ✹ ✹ ✹

Doctor, doctor, I keep thinking I'm a moth.
Get out of the way, you're in my light.

WAITER, WAITER

Waiter, waiter! There's a fly in my soup.
What do you expect for 50 cents, sir? A beetle?

Waiter, waiter! There's a flea in my soup.
Tell him to hop it.

Waiter, waiter! There's a fly in my soup!
Yes, sir, he's committed insecticide.

Waiter, waiter! There's a slug in my salad.
I'm sorry, sir, I didn't know you were a vegetarian.

Waiter, waiter! There's a fly in my custard.
I'll fetch him a spoon sir.

Waiter, waiter!
There's a slug
in my dinner.
Don't worry,
sir, there's no
extra charge.

Waiter, waiter! There's a cockroach on my steak.
They don't seem to care what they eat, do they sir?

— o — o — .

Waiter, waiter! There's a maggot in my salad.
Don't worry, he won't live long in that stuff.

— o — o — .

Waiter, waiter! There's a spider in my soup.
It's hardly deep enough to drown him, sir.

— o — o — .

Waiter, waiter! There's a slug in my lettuce.
Sorry madam, no pets allowed here.

— o — o — .

Waiter, waiter! There's a wasp in my pudding.
So that's where they go to in the winter.

— o — o — .

Waiter, waiter! There's a worm in my soup.
That's not a worm, sir, that's your sausage.

Waiter, waiter! There's a fly in my soup.
Yes, that's the manager, sir. The last customer was a witch doctor.

Waiter, waiter! There's a fly in my wine.
Well you did ask for something with a little body, sir.

Waiter, waiter! My lunch is talking to me!
Well you asked for a tongue sandwich, sir.

Waiter, waiter! There's a fly in my soup.
Yes, madam, it's the bad meat that attracts them.

Waiter, waiter! What's this dead fly doing on my meat?
I don't know, madam, it must have died after tasting it.

Waiter, waiter! There's a spider in my soup. Send for the manager!
It's no good, sir, he's frightened of them too.

Waiter, waiter! Do you serve snails.
Sit down, sir, we'll serve anyone.

Waiter, waiter! Have you got frogs legs?
No, sir, I always walk like this.

Waiter, waiter, do you have frogs' legs?
Yes sir.
Well then hop into the kitchen for my soup.

✗   ✗   ✗

Waiter, waiter, can I have frog's legs?
Well I suppose you could but you'd need surgery!

✗   ✗   ✗

Waiter, waiter, are there snails on the menu?
Why yes, sir, they must have escaped from the kitchen.

✗   ✗   ✗

Waiter, waiter! What's this spider doing in my alphabet soup?
Probably learning to read sir.

✗   ✗   ✗

Waiter, waiter! There's a beetle in my soup.
Sorry sir, we're out of flies today.

✗   ✗   ✗

Waiter, waiter! There's a mosquito in my soup.
Don't worry sir, mosquitoes have very small appetites.

Waiter, waiter! There's a dead
fly in my soup.
Yes sir, it's the heat that kills
them.

Waiter, waiter! There's a fly
in the butter.
Yes sir, it's a butterfly.

Waiter, waiter! There's a fly
in my soup.
Don't panic sir. I'll call the
animal sanctuary.

Waiter, waiter! There's a fly in my soup!
Don't worry sir, the spider in your bread will get it.

Waiter, waiter! There's a bee in my alphabet soup.
Yes, sir, and I hope there's an A and C and all the other letters too.

Waiter, waiter! There are two flies in my soup.
That's all right sir. Have the extra one on me.

Waiter, waiter! What's this spider doing in my soup?
Trying to save the fly from drowning by the look of it, sir.

Waiter, waiter! There's a spider in my salad.
Yes sir, the chef's using Webb lettuces today.

365

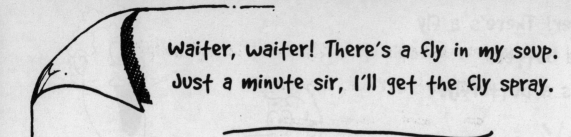

Waiter, waiter! There's a fly in my soup.
Just a minute sir, I'll get the fly spray.

___

Waiter, waiter! There's a hair in my soup?
Is it brown or purple? We seem to have lost a monster somewhere.

___

Waiter, waiter! Could I have a mammoth steak please?
With pleasure, sir.
No, with ketchup please.

___

Waiter, waiter! I can't eat this meat, it's crawling with maggots.
Quick, run to the other end of the table, you can catch it as it goes by.

___

Waiter, waiter! There's a dead fly in my soup.
Oh no! Who's going to look after his family?

___

Waiter, waiter! What's this cockroach doing on my ice-cream sundae?
I think it's skiing downhill.

___

Waiter, waiter! There's a slug in my lettuce.
Quiet, they'll all want one.

Waiter, waiter! What's this fly doing in my soup?
Breast stroke, madam.

▭ ▭ ▭ ▭

Waiter, waiter! There's a teeny beetle in my broccoli.
I'll see if I can find a bigger one madam.

▭ ▭ ▭ ▭

Waiter, waiter! There's a fly in my soup.
Go ahead and eat him. There are plenty more where he came from.

▭ ▭ ▭ ▭

Sir, you haven't touched your custard.
No, I'm waiting for the fly to stop using it as a trampoline.

▭ ▭ ▭ ▭

Waiter, waiter! What's this cockroach doing in my soup?
We ran out of flies.

▭ ▭ ▭ ▭

Waiter, waiter! There's a fly in my soup!
Just wait until you see the main course.

Waiter, waiter! There's a dead fly
swimming in my soup.
Nonsense sir, dead flies can't swim.

Waiter, waiter! There's a fly
in my bean soup.
Don't worry sir, I'll take
it back and exchange it
for a bean.

Waiter, waiter! What's this creepy crawly thing doing in my lettuce?
I think he's trying to get out, madam.

Watier, waiter! What's this creepy crawly thing doing in my dinner?
Oh, that one – he comes here every night.

Waiter, waiter! What's this creepy crawly thing doing
waltzing round my table?
It's the band, sir, it's playing his tune.

Waiter, waiter! What's this
creepy crawly thing doing
on my wife's shoulder?
I don't know –
friendly
thing isn't he?

Waiter, waiter!
There's a fly in my starter.
Get rid of it would you?
I can't do that, sir,
he hasn't had his main
course yet.

Waiter, waiter, what's this fly
doing on my ice-cream?
Looks like he's learning to ski, sir.

Waiter, waiter! What's this fly
doing in my ice cream?
Maybe he likes winter sports.

Waiter, waiter!
There's a frog in my soup.
Don't worry, madam, there's not
enough there to drown him.

Waiter, waiter! There's a fly in my soup.
And what's the problem sir?
I ordered slug soup.

Waiter, waiter! Did you know there is a fly in my soup?
That's not a fly sir, it's just dirt in the shape of a fly.

Waiter, waiter! What's this fly doing in my soup?
I think it's drowning sir.

Why do waiters prefer monsters to flies?
Have you ever heard anyone complaining of a monster in their soup?

STORIES

Two fleas were sitting on Robinson Crusoe's back. one hopped off saying "Byee! See you on friday!"

Two ants were watching a useless golfer swing wildly, trying to hit the ball. one said to the other, "come on, let's get on the ball before he hits us."

A mother moth was telling her baby moth off saying, "If you don't eat all your cotton, you won't get any satin."

Two mosquitoes were buzzing round when they saw a drunken man. one said to the other "You bite him — I'm driving."

A flea jumped over the swinging doors of a saloon, drank three whiskeys and jumped out again. He picked himself up from the dirt, dusted himself down and said, "ok, who moved my dog?"

Two weevils came to town from the country. one worked hard and became very rich. The other became the lesser of two weevils.

A very posh lady was walking around an art gallery when she stopped by one particular exhibit. "I suppose this picture of a hideous witch is what you would call modern art," she said very pompously.
"No madam," replied the assistant, "it's what we call a mirror."

A witch went into a sweet shop to buy some sweets. The man behind the counter said "Gosh you are really ugly aren't you? I've never seen anyone as offensively hideous as you." "Young man" she replied, "I didn't come in here to be insulted." "Really," he said, "where do you usually go?"

A man visited a friend's home for the first time and was let in by a very ugly woman. In the living room he asked the friend, "was that witch who let me in your wife?" "of course," replied his friend, "do you think I'd have a maid that ugly?"

371

Little Johnny and his mother were on a train. Johnny leant over and started to whisper in his mother's ear. "Johnny, how many times have I told you," said his mother, "it's rude to whisper. If you have something to say, say it out loud."

"All right," said Johnny, "why does the lady opposite look like an ugly, haggard old witch?"

A witch went into a beauty parlor and asked the assistant how much it would cost to make her look like a film star. "Nothing" replied the assistant. "Nothing?" she said, "But how can I look like a film star?"

"Haven't you seen a film called *The Creature from the Black Lagoon*," replied the assistant.

A big-mouthed, green, warty toad lived in a slimy swamp. He was a very friendly toad and enjoyed meeting other creatures in the swamp. one day he met a two-headed python. "Hello, what are you?" he asked.

"I'm a two-headed python" replied the snake.

"Great! I'm a big-mouthed, green warty toad - good to meet you!" Then the next day he met an ugly, big warthog. "Hello, what are you?" he asked.

"I'm an ugly, big warthog," said the creature.

"Great! I'm a big-mouthed, green, warty toad!" he replied.

Then just the next day he met a huge, furry Yeti.

"Hello, what are you?" he asked.

"I'm a huge, furry Yeti and I eat big-mouthed, green, warty toads," said the creature.

The toad pursed his lips together very small and whispered, "Hm, you don't see many of those around do you?"

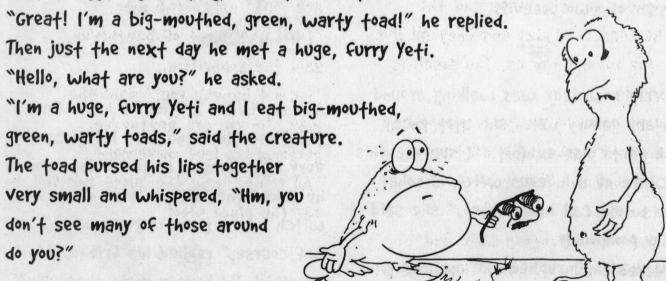

A workman had just finished laying a carpet in a witch's house when he realized he had lost his sandwiches. Looking round he saw a lump under the carpet. Not wanting to pull the carpet up again he just got a bit plank of wood and smashed the lump flat. Then the witch came into the room with a cup of tea for him. "Here's your tea," she said. "My you've laid that carpet well. Just one thing, though, have you seen my pet toad anywhere?"

A wizard went to the doctor one day complaining of headaches. "It's because I live in the same room as two of my brothers," he said. "one of them has six goats and the other has four pigs and they all live in the room with us. The smell is terrible."

"Well, couldn't you just open the windows?" asked the doctor.

"certainly not," he replied, "my bats would fly out."

A snake went into a cafe and ordered a cup of tea. "That will be $4," said the waitress, "and may I say that it's nice to see you here. We don't get many snakes coming in here."

"I'm not surprised at $4 for a cup of tea!" he replied.

Two witches lost their brooms and crash-landed on an iceberg. "Do you think we'll be here long?" asked the first.

"No," said the second, "here comes the Titanic."

A man came home from work one day to find a ghostly figure with lots of wild hair, a long, ragged jacket and big staring eyes. "Who are you?" asked the man.

"I am the ghost of Beethoven," said the apparition.

"I don't believe you," said the man, "if you are Beethoven, perform his last movement."

"All right," said the ghost and fell off the piano stool.

A ghost was sitting in a haunted house all alone when another ghost came in. It said, "Hello, I'm your long lost brother."

The first ghost said "ooooo?"

Two wizards in a car were driving along and the police were chasing them for speeding. one said "What are we going to do?"

The other replied, "Quick, turn the car into a side street."

A Cannibal caught a missionary in the jungle. "Now how shall I cook you?" said the cannibal, "are you best roasted or broiled?"

"To tell you the truth," replied the missionary, "I'm a friar."

A butler came running into his important master's office. "Sir, sir, there's a ghost in the Corridor. What shall I do with him?"

Without looking up from his work the master said, "Tell him I can't see him."

Two cannibals were having their tea. one said to the other "I don't like your friend."

The other one said, "Well put him to one side and just eat the greens."

Two girls were having their packed lunch in the school playground. one had an apple and the other said, "Watch out for worms won't you!"
The first one replied "Why should I? They can watch out for themselves."

Two monster-hunters tracked a huge, slobbering monster with enormous fangs in the jungle. All they had were two sticks each. one said to the other "You go for him. I'll keep you covered."

Some vampires went to see Dracula. They said "Drac, we want to open a zoo. Have you got any advice?"
"Yes," replied Dracula, "have lots of giraffes."

Some more vampires went to see Dracula. They said, "Drac, we're going to start a football team."
"Great," he said, "I'll be ghoulie."
They said, "When we've had a bit of practice we'll challenge the human beings to a game."
Dracula said, "Be careful, the stakes will be high."
They said, "No, we've got this brilliant idea. We'll have these very long games which'll tire them out. The first half will run from dusk to midnight and the second half from midnight till dawn."
Dracula said, "And what happens if it goes to extra time?"

A ghost came home one night and his wife said "Are you drunk again?"
He said, "No of course, not. How dare you!"
She replied, "Well you look legless."

Two men were having a drink together. one said, "I'd rather live with a vampire than with my wife."

"Why's that?" asked the other.

He said, "Because she's always trying to bite my head off."

———— o ————

A man tried to poison his wife. As she lay writhing on the floor saying, "what have I done? What have I done? What have you put in my tea?"

He said, "oh shut up! There you go, belly-aching again!"

— · — · — · —

The man tried to poison his wife again. This time she lay on the floor shouting "wretch, wretch, wretch!"

He said, "No, you retch - you took the poison."

〰〰〰〰〰〰

The sheriff looked at the man with a noose around his neck and said, "I'll tell you what, I'm going to give you a suspended sentence."

The man said,

"Thank you, thank you, thank you."

The sheriff said,

"Right boys, hang him!"

A man was sitting in the electric chair. The executioner said, "Look, I'm sorry but I'm going to have to throw the switch in a minute." The man said, "Do us a favor and throw it out of the window!"

Frankenstein was sitting in his cell when suddenly through the wall came the ghost of his monster, with a rope round his neck. Frankenstein said, "Monster, monster, what are you doing here?" The monster said, "Well boss, they hanged me this morning so now I've come to meet my maker."

Two spiders were sitting on a web. one of them said, "See that fly up there. He's never flown before." The other one said, "What's that got to do with you?" The first one said, "I'm trying to talk him down."

The man who was about to die said to the sheriff, "Say, do I really have to die swinging from a tree?" "course not," replied the Sheriff, "we just put the rope round your neck and kick the horse away. After that it's up to you."

Two teenage boys were talking in the classroom. one said, "I took my girlfriend to see *The Bride of Dracula* last night." "oh yeah," said the other, "what was she like?"
"well she was about six foot six, white as a ghost and she had big red staring eyes and fangs."
The other said, "Yes, but what was *The Bride of Dracula* like?"

A man was staying in a big old country house and in the middle of the night he met a ghost. The ghost said, "I have been walking these corridors for 300 years."
The man said, "In that case, can you tell me the way to the toilet?"

A woman went to the fridge to get some milk and all she found was a disembodied hand. It was all fingers and thumbs.

A little demon came home from school one day and said to his mother, "I hate my sister's guts." "All right," said his mother, "I won't put them in your sandwiches again."

The story goes that some students of charles Darwin glued together parts from several different kinds of insects, and took the composite insect to Darwin for identification. When Darwin looked at the insect, he asked the students if it hummed when it was alive. They said that it did. Darwin said, "Then it must be a humbug."

Each silkworm in a colony bet on a boast:
That its silk production would be the most.
But none of them won – and the reason why?
All the silk they made wound up in a tie.
(or maybe it wound up in a shirt.)

Mr and Mrs Hill and their three children were on a touring holiday in Transylvania where they stopped for the night in Dracula's castle. That night, the evil count sucked the blood out of all of them and put them in coffins in his vaults. The next night Dracula sat by the organ thundering out loud music, while down in the cellar the poor Hills stirred in their coffins. They made their way up to the organ gallery and when Dracula saw them he said, "Welcome to the vampire club. This next song is especially for you." And with that he began to play *The Hills are Alive With the Sound of Music.*

A blind rabbit and a blind snake ran into each other on the road one day. The snake reached out, touched the rabbit and said, "You're soft and fuzzy and have floppy ears. You must be a rabbit."
The rabbit reached out, touched the snake and said "You're slimy, beady-eyed and low to the ground. You must be a math teacher."

A reporter was captured by some cannibals in the jungle and taken back to the camp where he was prepared for the chief's supper. "What do you do in England?" asked the cook as he was about to light the fire.
"I was an editor," replied the journalist.

"You'll soon be editor-in-chief," said the cook.

When a plane caught fire over the jungle, the pilot ejected and landed in a cannibal's pot. The cannibal turned to his friend and said, "What's this flier doing in my soup?"

The cannibal priest told his flock to close their eyes and say grace. "For whosoever we are about to eat, may the Lord make us truly thankful."

Two cannibals were walking along the road when they passed a line of people waiting for a bus. "Oh look," said one of them, "a barbequeue."

A frog walked into a library and asked the librarian what he would recommend. "How about this, sir?" asked the librarian, showing him *Toad of Toad Hall*.
"Reddit, reddit," said the frog.

A woman walked into a pet shop and said, "I'd like a frog for my son."
"Sorry madam," said the shopkeeper, "we don't do part exchange."

A man walked into a pub and said, "Does anyone here own a large cat with a pointy head?"
Everyone shook their heads. "Oh, no," he said, "I must have just run over a witch!"

A little boy came running into the kitchen. "Dad, Dad," he said, "there's a monster at the door with a really ugly face."
"Tell him you've already got one," said his father.

A cannibal was walking through the jungle when he came to a clearing and saw a freshly-killed elephant lying down, with a pygmy standing on top of it brandishing a big stick and doing a victory dance. "Have you just killed that elephant?" asked the cannibal.
"Yes," replied the pygmy, "I did it with my club."
"Wow," said the cannibal, "you must have a really big club!"
"Yes," replied the pygmy, "there are about 40 of us in it!"

Two policemen in New York were watching King Kong climb up the Empire State Building. One said to the other "What do you think he's doing?" "It's obvious," replied his colleague, "he wants to catch a plane."

Two bees were flying over the same garden. When they had passed it one said to the other, "Hey, you know there's a man and a woman down there with flowers growing out of their bottoms."
The other said, "How do you know that?"
The first one said, "I looked in my rear view mirror."

Some kids were going round a museum when they came to a tiny skeleton. They said to the curator, "Whose skeleton's that?"
"Oliver Cromwell's," replied the man.
"It's not!" they replied, "Oliver Cromwell was a big man!"
"Er, yes," replied the curator, "that's right. But this is his skeleton when he was a little boy."

oliver cromwell

A lady put a lonely hearts ad in the paper and had a reply which said, "I would love to meet you but I have to tell you that I am eight feet tall, covered in matted fur, with large fangs and slobbering lips. If you still want to meet me then I'll be under the clock in the market square at six o'clock next Saturday."

The lady replied, "I would be interested in meeting you but please will you wear a red carnation and carry a rolled-up copy of The Times so that I can recognize you?"

A monster goes to a gas station and says, "fill me up."
The gas man replies, "You have to have a car for me to do that!"
The monster replies, "But I had a car for lunch!"

Three men are walking along the beach one day when they see a cave. The first man goes in and is just looking at a banknote on a big rock when a ghostly voice calls out "I am the ghost of Auntie Mabel and this five dollars stays on the table!" The second man goes in and is reaching for the note when the same thing happens again. The third man goes in, sees the five dollars and cries out "I am the ghost of Davy Crockett and this five dollars goes in my pocket!"

Two owls were playing pool. one said "Two hits."
The other replied "Two hits to who?"

Johnny collected lots of money from trick or treating and he went to the sweetshop to buy some chocolate. "You should give that money to charity," said the shopkeeper. Johnny thought for a moment and said, "No, I'll buy the chocolate. You give the money to charity."

A man was fishing in the jungle. After a while another angler came to join him. "Have you had any bites?" asked the second man. "Yes, lots," replied the first one, "but they were all mosquitoes."

Two boys were walking through a churchyard one dark and stormy night. As one stopped to do up his shoelaces they heard an eerie voice coming from behind one of the tombs saying "Now that I've got you I'm going to eat your legs first, then your arms, then your head and finally I'll gulp down your body." Terrified, the boys ran for the exit but before they could get out of the gate a figure in black loomed before them. "I thought I heard someone," said the vicar, "would you boys like a jelly baby?"

one day a boy was walking down the street when he saw a sea monster standing on the corner looking lost. The boy put a lead on the sea monster and took him to the police station.

"You should take him to the museum," said the police sergeant. The next day the police sergeant saw the boy in the town still with the monster on a lead.

"I thought I told you to take him to the museum," said the policeman.

"I did," said the boy, "and today I'm taking him to the cinema."

Two monsters went duck-hunting with their dogs but without success. "I know what we're doing wrong," said the first one.

"What's that then?" said the second.

"We're not throwing the dogs high enough!"

THE END

CHILDREN'S BOOKS AVAILABLE FROM
ROBINSON PUBLISHING

The Biggest Joke Book in the World   *Tom & Matt Keegan*   £6.99
All the jokes you will ever need to know.

The Joke Museum
   Sandy Ransford   £3.99
A collection of the finest, funniest and oldest jokes in the world.

The Big Bad Joke Book
   Zig and Zag   £3.99
Zig and Zag present over 1,000 fantastic jokes.

1001 Knock Knock Jokes
   Jasmine Birtles   £3.99
All the old favorites as well as hilarious new ones.

**The Ultimate Book of
Unforgettable Creepy Crawly
Jokes**
   Liz Hughes   £6.99
Jokes about everything from slugs and mosquitoes, bees and bats to creepy ghouls and witches' cats.

1001 Animal Quacker Jokes
   Jasmine Birtles   £3.99
There are jokes in here for every animal you can imagine – and some you can't!

The Biggest Book of Stupid Jokes in the Universe   *David Mostyn*   £6.99
Jam-packed with a spectacular selection of the most incredibly stupid – but hilariously funny – jokes.

The Puzzle Factory   *Sue Preston*   £3.99
The ultimate puzzle challenge, which will keep even the brightest minds occupied for hours.

Horse Stories   *Felicity Trotman*   £4.99
More than thirty of the best tales ever written about horses, riders and riding.

Dance Stories   *Felicity Trotman*   £4.99
Wonderful collection of exciting, glamorous and romantic stories about the world of dance.

Fantasy Stories *Mike Ashley* £4.99

Some of the best fantasy stories of the century. Many have been written especially for this book, others are classics.

Space Stories *Mike Ashley* £4.99

Around thirty exciting stories, some set on a future Earth, others on worlds far away.

True Mystery Stories *Finn Bevan* £4.99

Collection of thirty tales based on the world's most fascinating unexplained phenomena.

True Sea Stories *Paul Aston* £4.99

Tales of mystery, crime and piracy, sunken treasure, races won and lost, and silent, deadly beasts beneath the waves.

True Horror Stories *Terrance Dicks* £4.99

More than thirty accounts of truly terrifying experiences, including the horror of a plane crash and of being trapped underground.

True Survival Stories *Anthony Masters* £4.99

Gripping tales of survival against all the odds, including Apollo 13, the Andes plane crash, and many more.

Robinson books are available from all good bookshops or can be ordered direct from the publisher. Just tick the title you want and fill in the form below.

Robinson Publishing Ltd, PO Box 11, Falmouth, Cornwall TR10 9EN
Tel: +44(0) 1326 317200 Fax: +44(0) 1326 317444 Email: books@Barni.avel.co.uk

UK/BFPO customers please allow £1.00 for p&p for the first book, plus 50p for the second, plus 30p for each additional book up to a maximum charge of £3.

Overseas customers (inc Ireland) please allow £2.00 for the first book, plus £1.00 for the second, plus 50p for each additional book.

Please send me the titles ticked above.

NAME (Block letters) ....

ADDRESS ....

.... POSTCODE ....

I enclose a cheque/PO (payable to Robinson Publishing Ltd) for ....
I wish to pay by Switch/Credit Card

.... Card Expiry Date ....